NARRATIVE BIOGRAPHIES OF THE BATDORF FAMILY GENEALOGY INCLUDING WERT, PETERS, ROW, WELKER, SWARTZ, SCHUPP, FRANTZ, STEINER, MESSERSCHMIDT, FABER, WERTZ, RUDY(3), GIESEMAN, WEISS, JURY, SCHROT, MILLER(2), GARMAN ET AL

MARC D. THOMPSON & JACK SMILES

OTHER BOOKS BY AUTHOR

Compendium of Virtual and Traditional Fitness, © 2015, 978-0-9908074-0-7

Fitness Book of Lists, © 2012, 978-0615656304

Fitness Quotes of Humorous Inspiration, © 2011, 978-0988344082

Genealogy of Anderson, Keefer, Gaugler, Livezly…, © 2014, 978-0988344037

Genealogy of Batdorf, Wert, Peters, Row..., © 2013, 978-0988344013

Genealogy of Duncan, Layman, McCloud, Overlander..., © 2014, 978-0988344020

Genealogy of Mazo, Curry, Thompson, Mason..., © 2010, 978-0988344075

Genealogy of Romano, Disimone, Vitale, Viviano..., © 2012, 9780988344068

Genealogy of Thompson, Hensel, Goodman, Updegrove…, © 2013, 978-0988344044

Genealogy of Wittle, Acri, Stewart, Barbuscio..., © 2011, 978-0988-44051

Narrative Biographies of the Anderson Family Genealogy, © 2014, 978-500225681

Narrative Biographies of the Duncan Family Genealogy, © 2014, 978-1500123598

Narrative Biographies of the Romano Family Genealogy, © 2014, 978-1500405243

Poems...Of Eternal Moments, © 2012, 978-0-988344082

Thompson Family History, Vol X, Ed 5, © 2014, 978-1499352719

Virtual Personal Training Manual, © 2013, 978-0-988344099

Family histories require constant revision. As this century moves along, more and more information becomes digitally or electronically disposable. If we do not save this information, it may be lost forever. Please contact author with any corrections or additions, marc@VirtuFit.net.

NARRATIVE BIOGRAPHIES OF THE BATDORF FAMILY GENEALOGY INCLUDING WERT, PETERS, ROW, WELKER, SWARTZ, SCHUPP, FRANTZ, STEINER, MESSERSCHMIDT, FABER, WERTZ, RUDY(3), GIESEMAN, WEISS, JURY, SCHROT, MILLER(2), GARMAN ET AL

ISBN: 978-0-9908074-1-4

MARC D. THOMPSON

Cover photograph Thomas Batdorf & Mary Peters *c*1910

www.VirtuFit.net - marc@VirtuFit.net

This volume is dedicated to all our family and friends, who selflessly donated information, time, effort, research and love to make this compilation possible.

ACKNOWLEDGMENTS

Thanks to my parents, to my sisters, to Joe from Pennsylvania State Library and to my hundreds of cousins who have selflessly donated their hard–worked family histories. Thanks to every clerk and registrar, cemetery manager and LDS employee, ancestry.com staff, who have taken their time to assist in discovering our roots. This book is truly the love of thousands.

TABLE OF CONTENTS

FOREWORD

by Cynthia Welker-Maloney

I, like Marc D. Thompson, am a direct descendent of our Valentine Welker born about January11, 1755 in Frankenthal. Valentine came to America on the ship Crawford, arriving in Philadelphia and gave his oath of allegiance in 1772 in Philadelphia. According to Early Pa Marriages, Valentine met and married Susannah Jory, the daughter of Abraham Shora and his wife Catherine Guerne, in Lykens Valley in 1783.

In my years of researching, I have met the most nicest and helpful unrelated and related people. The motto of a family historian is always keep researching for we are all related somehow and we are all family. Marc was one of my first contacts over fifteen years ago when I began my journey. We are lucky to have someone with Marc's credentials and expertise compile and publishing this information.

PREFACE

by Marc D. Thomspon

If I were given the opportunity to live in any era, I would most certainly pick the 1870s. The time was simple and the people were honest. Folks worked hard and took pride in their families, their homes and their reputations. When I look into the eyes of our ancestors from that time period, I feel a link; I would have fit nicely in their time.

Genealogy was created in order for people to know the history of their lineage, to discover their origins, and to prove bloodlines and royalty. This volume was compiled in response to their deep desire to understand and discover their past. It shall stand as part of the legacy of their ancestry. They have remembrances. They have goals, glories, and personalities. The Irish kings would pass down their regal history orally. They would recite a list of names—their kin—noting outstanding events associated with the forebearers. The ancient Scottish bards similarly memorized their royal families, reciting the pedigrees of the Old Scot's Kings regardless of the complexity.

Our 35-year journey of knowledge has led to a plethora of information. We have learned much. We have discovered our roots—good, bad, and ugly. It has molded us. It has given us information on our health and ways to stay fit and healthy. It has given us photographs, the opportunity to see ourselves in generations gone by, noting how our features and personalities have evolved. It has helped with our jobs, our relationships, our lives. Our ancestors are a mirror of ourselves that can aide in our survival and understanding. Ancestry is wisdom.

We have discovered that we are related to some famous and infamous folks, and even found that there are some areas of the country named for our distant families. We are direct-line descendants of King Philip of France and the Royal families Cleves. We are descended from WWII servicemen: Ed Mazo, Percy C Forsythe and Robert J Forsythe. WWI serviceman: Raymond F Barbush. Civil War servicemen: Andrew G. Hensel, Cyrus Shannon, Daniel Updegrove, Elijah Anderson, Jacob H Wittle, John E Shover, John H Minnick, Sebastian Shover and Thomas E. Batdorf. War of 1812 servicemen: Adam Frantz, Andrew W. Hensel and Joseph Workman. Revolutionary War servicemen: Andrew Messerschmidt, Andrew Miller, John Casper Hensel, Frank Row, Henry W Bucher, Jacob Lehman, Jacob Livezey, Jacob Philip Bordner, Jacob Rudy, John Adam Guise, John Balthaser Romberger, John Conrad Bucher, John Daniel Angst, John Faber, John George Schupp, John Miller, John Peter Shaffer, Jonas Rudy, Michael Garman, Michael Layman, Nicholas Mantz, Peter Braun (British), Peter Keefer, Valentine Welker and William Anderson. World Mayors: John Guerne and John Emmerich, and Religious leaders John Peter Batdorf, John Batdorf, John George Bager Jr., John George Bager Sr., John Heilferich Lotz and George Gaukel; and entrepreneur Alexander Thompson.

We are direct-line descendants of some of the famous homesteads and locations, including the George Bager Homestead, Abbottstown, PA; the Chris Miller Homestead, North Lebanon Township, PA; the George Mennig (Minnich) Homestead, PA; the Thomas Benfield homestead, Berks Co., PA; the Livesey Homestead, Philadelphia, PA; and the Wirth Homestead, Lykens Valley Golf Course, Dauphin Co., PA (demolished 1989). Additionally, our ancestors' names were immortalized at these locations: Bordnersville, Kelly Crossroads, Livesey Street, Herrold's Island, Keefer's Station, Deibler's Gap, Deibler's Dam, and Shoemakertown, all in Pennsylvania.

Finally, our ancestors had surnames named after the Jura Mountains of Switzerland and Acri, Italy, among other locations. We are collateral descendants of Presidents Dwight D. Eisenhower and William McKinley and Pennsylvania politicians Samuel Pennypacker, John Morton, and Jonas Row. Civil War Brigadier General Galushia Pennypacker, entertainers Marlon Brando, Les Brown, and Ray W Brown; religious leaders Conrad Weiser and Michael Enderline; Melba Dodge, Jesse Runkle, Enrico Caruso, and Galla Curci are all cousins. Last, Taylor Wittel lists relations to James Madison, Zachary Taylor, Jefferson Davis, and Gene Autry

At the moment, our paternal line breaks down to about 11/16 German, 2/16 Scottish, 1/16 French, 1/16 Swiss, 1/32 English, and 1/32 Dutch-Bohemian. Our maternal line breaks down to about 10/16 German, 4/16 UK, 1/16 French, 1/32 Swiss and 1/32 Scandanavian. The approximate percentages of relatives born in these area are: 45% born in Pennsylvania, 17% born in Germany, 14% born in Scotland, 9% born in Italy, 4% born in Georgia, 4% born in South Carolina, 4% born in Ireland, 2% born in New York, and 1% born in Virginia, Florida, Switzerland, England, Bohemia, France, Sweden, Finland, and the West Indies.

This volume will serve to honor us with the researched and documented information of our background. Our ancestry was derived from this data—the Thompson Family History (TFH) genealogy—which includes:

8,041	Relatives in TFH
5,500	Sources checked
2,307	Marriages in TFH

1410	Oldest birthdate: Geoffrey Livesay
1,279	Places in TFH
1,169	Sources used
1,111	Surnames in TFH
1,084	Direct-line ancestors, all children
549	Direct-line ancestors, author
515	Media records in TFH
94	Age at death: Sarah Faber, Mchl Goodman, Ursula Buglio, and Mrs. M. Curcio
85	Ancestors named same male nam: John, Johannes, Jean, etc
82	Ancestors named Sophia or Maria
74	Ancestors named same female name: Mary, Maria, Mary Ann, etc.
68	Oldest age males having children: James McKinsey and Alexander Thompson
50+	Most variations for single surname: Batdorf, Bodorff, Batterff, Pottorf, etc.
49	Oldest age females having children: numerous women
34	Ancestors named Shirley or Mary
27	Number of letters of longest female: Amelia Dorothy Elizabeth Bager
24	Number of letters of longest male: Howard Andrew Carson Hensel
21	Ancestors named Connor (1) or Adam (20)
21	Generations discovered: Livesay
21	Youngest death: Margaret Muckle
17	Ancestors named Andrew (16) or Roman (1)
15	Youngest age male having child: John E Shover
14	Youngest age female having child: Anna Maria Hamm
11	Number of countries ancestors born
8	Most different ancestral lines with same surname: Miller, Mueller, etc.
7	Number of states ancestors born in: PA, NY, DE, GA, SC, VA, FL
3	Ancestors who died at sea: N. Benesch, G. Reith & G. Shoemaker
2	Ancestors named Ashley (1) or Renae (1)
2	Ancestors named Gerald or Gilbert

Many genealogies tend to trace a descendant line or the paternal line (single ascendancy). Our purpose was to trace all ancestors with equal perseverance. This is a monumental—if not impossible—task. We have compiled a pedigree, beginning with our children and using an ahnentafel format. Our children are generation 1, their parents are generation 2, their grandparents are generation 3, etc. There is a family group sheet for each pair of parents along the pedigree. The emphasis at present is on generations 1 through 10, although we have completed research as far back as generation

20. Additional collateral ancestors have begun to be added as of 2014.

In most cases, the Anglicized first and middle names were used throughout the TFH. For example, Johann Heinrich is John Henry and Orsala Francesca is Ursula Frances. The most commonly found surname was used, whether Anglicized or not. The majority of the collateral information was derived from the U.S. Census records. To preserve privacy, all information on living persons has been removed or privatized.

The continued excellence of this genealogy will be improved through the following plan.

 A. Correct errors and complete source citations.
 B. Collect photographs and medical history of ancestors.
 C. Document more personal information of ancestors leading to a more biographical history of family.
 D. Expound on current family group sheets and extend parentage.
 E. Continue the written biographical volumes (narratives).
 F. Begin documenting the descendant lines.

I have a desire and I have a bond. I have a desire to know from whence we came. I want to know our history, our origins. I want to know what our ancestors did, how they persevered and how the spark of life made its way from Geoffrey Livesay, born 1410 in England, to Sophia, born 2004 in Florida. I feel that bond. I have a strong connection to the late 19th century. As this century moves along, more and more information becomes digitally or electronically disposable. If we do not save this information, it may be lost forever. The Thompson Family History is a guide for future generations who may use this information for their own goals, whatever they may be. We have given our children a foundation. Take it, improve it, embrace it. Read and enjoy.

INTRODUCTION

by Marc D. Thompson

As Malcolm Gladwell says, "Who we are cannot be separated from where we're from." Genealogy is a duty. The day we were born or the day we bore children ourselves, we gained a responsibility of passing along our history. We are responsible for the knowledge of our parents and of our grandparents and all the wisdom that comes with this knowledge. Our duty, therefore, includes our children's heritage—including the names and faces of their forefathers and mothers, the medical history and genetic backgrounds of their blood lines, the princes and the paupers, the photographs and historical areas and properties, the tragedies and the joys.

These Thompson Family History (TFH) narratives are our heritage, and with this information we can be proud of ourselves and our past, and aim toward a bright future and better lives. If our duty is neglected, as each generation passes so will our family history.

The mission of our genealogy books is to document and record all that is available of our ancestors and reap the enjoyment that these discoveries bring. The first goal is to amass photographs—as a face can tell a thousand tales—so much can be learned from them. The second goal of our research is to document the medical background of our ancestors so our children can lead a healthier life.

The third goal is to continue to extend the lineage in order to link to as many others as possible. Our ancestors are not mere names or dates—they have tales to tell, journeys to document, lives for us to discover. They have accomplishments and setbacks. Therefore our final goal leads us to the building of narratives from this amassed information, producing a readable experience of our ancestors and their lives. This is one of several narrative genealogies produced from the amazing amount of documented data. As we mentioned "Who we are cannot be separated from where we're from," this book therefore allows us to better understand ourselves and our families via our ancestors.

CHAPTER 1

JAMES EDWARD BATDORF
&
BEULAH IRENE WERT

JAMES EDWARD BATDORF & BEULAH IRENE WERT

Having been born in Loyalton, Dauphin County, Pennsylvania, in 1885, James Edward Batdorf had little control over his fate. In an area where nearly all employment was tied directly or indirectly to the world's largest deposits of anthracite coal, he became a coal miner. Loyalton is an unincorporated community within Washington Township and it's likely that James went to one of the nine one-room schoolhouses in Washington Township, and dropped out after the equivalent of eighth grade to go to work. According to a 1900 Bureau of Mines report, 363 collieries in the anthracite region employed 143,826 workers, one-fourth of them boys under sixteen.

Though deep-mining anthracite coal was tough and dangerous work—anthracite mine accidents in Eastern Pennsylvania in 1900 killed 411, injured 1,057, and made 230 widows and 525 orphans—it also offered substantial pay. A certified miner could earn twice the national average 1910 pay of $750 a year. To be certified, a miner had to pass a test in English, buy his own tools and equipment, and hire his own laborers (or butties).

Anthracite is the highest grade of coal in the earth. Anthracite burns cleaner, hotter, and four times longer than bituminous and is virtually smoke free, while bituminous combustion emits a sooty black smoke. The anthracite coal mined in Eastern Pennsylvania fueled iron blast furnaces for the production of high-grade steel, drove railroads, and heated homes. The U.S. Navy especially coveted anthracite. The heat gave warships speed and the lack of smoke gave them stealth.

At 5'6'' and about 145 pounds as an adult, James Batdorf was an ideal size for deep mining work. He was a family man, good friend, and a public servant. In January of 1906, when he was nineteen, he went to the state capital of Harrisburg to be a pallbearer for a family friend of his sister Frances's finance Samuel Lutz. In August of that year James attended the marriage of his sister and Lutz in his parents' home, where he still lived. Pastor Brown of the Evangelical Church performed the wedding of Frances and Samuel and they departed immediately to honeymoon in Atlantic City.

James and Frances were two of seventeen children born to Thomas and Mary Louisa Peters Batdorf, both of whom were born in Dauphin County, Pennsylvania. Thomas was the descendant of Batdorfs who were among the Palatines, so-called because they emigrated from Palatinate, a region in southwestern Germany, due to economic devastation and religious persecution following the Thirty Years War that occurred from 1618 to 1638 in Central Europe, Those immigrants spoke a German dialect that became the Pennsylvania Dutch language still spoken today by the Amish.

Four of Thomas and Mary's children—Alvin, George, Kirby, and Norman—died in childhood. The other twelve—Verna, Stella, Cora, Harvey, Joseph, Frances, Oscar, James, Adam, Mary Ellen, William, and John—lived into adulthood.

In 1908, James, twenty-three, married Beulah Wert, nineteen. Though James, as his father had, went by his middle name Edward in his day-to-day life, when he was mentioned in local newspapers, such as when he ran as a Republican for inspector of elections in 1917, he was always James. James and Beulah settled in Washington

Township to live next to her parents—John Wert, born in neighboring Northumberland County, and Adeline Row, born in Dauphin County.

In the 1910 census the Werts and Batdorfs lived right next door to one another. The 1920 census shows both families moved to State Road in Washington Township, and again James and Beulah lived next door to her parents' home, which was described as a farm. The 1920 census also shows John and Adeline had a grandson, John Schiffer, living with them. As James and Beulah had five of their eventual six children by then—Alvin Leroy, Margaret Irene, Mildred Catherine, Harry Franklin and Myrtle Adeline—it's likely they moved to a bigger home. Romaine came later. James and Beulah were counted in the 1930 and the 1940 census, having moved to Lykens Borough, adjacent to Washington Township.

Beulah was born in 1889 in Elizabethville, just five miles southwest of Loyalton, where James was born. Both towns are in the Lykens Valley between the Mahantango and Berry ranges of the Appalachian Mountain range, an idyllic setting of rolling pastures and quaint towns set off by green mountains turning red and gold in the fall and gradually climbing to 1,500 to 2,000 feet.

Beulah was the fifth of six siblings of John and Adeline Row Wert, coming after Caroline ("Carrie"), Harriet ("Hattie"), a third child about whom nothing is known, and Florence. Beulah was the fifth child, followed by her sister Margaret. Beulah's work ethic was as strong as her husband's. She did most of the child rearing, kept the house, worked the family's garden, and was also a skilled dressmaker. In 1950, at the age of sixty-one, she was working hanging wallpaper.

Growing industries, railroads, and WWI kept the demand for coal high during the 1910s and 1920s—thus James and Beulah thrived. About 1922, the family bought its first automobile, a Ford Model T. They found plenty of recreation in the Lykens Valley with home-based card parties, church picnics, hiking clubs, and colliery competitions with baseball and tug of war games. Visiting family and friends was a pastime. The area was well connected by rail and in 1911, when James's brother Harvey visited his parents at Elizabethville, it was a news item in the Harrisburg Patriot's Nearby Towns section. A card party held by a Beatrice Batdorf at Lykens was also news.

Baseball and bowling were popular pastimes. Lykens and Elizabethville both had teams in the Twin County baseball league. A man named Batdorf, no first name given, was one of the top bowlers in the Allison Hill (east of Harrisburg) league. An F. Batdorf played basketball for the Wiconisco (adjacent to Lykens) High School team in the early 1920s. It is not known if James was a ballplayer or bowler, but it's likely he participated in colliery games

When the anthracite industry waned in the 1930s due to the Depression, James continued working as a road construction laborer with the Work Progress Administration and later for Lykens Borough, and was still working when he died in 1954 at age sixty-nine. Beulah survived him by twenty-nine years, living to her late nineties. They are buried side by side at Calvary United Methodist in Wiconisco.

Notes taken by Marc D. Thompson during an interview with James' and Beulah's daughter Mildred when she was eighty-eight gives a glimpse of what life was like in the Lykens Valley during part of James' and Beulah's life.

Mildred was born Mildred Catherine Batdorf on January 29, 1911, the daughter of Beulah Wert and James "Edward" Batdorf. She was the sister of my grandmother Myrtle, Alvin, Margaret, Harry, Ruth, and Romaine. Mildred and Myrtle were born and raised in Big Run, Pennsylvania. Their mother, Beulah, was the daughter of John and Adeline Wert of Big Run. The Wert family farmed and "were hard-working people." James Edward was the son of Thomas and Mary Batdorf, also of Big Run. Their "grandmother Batdorf was a housewife and grandfather Batdorf was a farmer and worked in the mines." Myrtle and Mildred "lived in a two-story house and ate in the kitchen." Their home was heated by coal and they did not have a fireplace. The family did not always have electricity, as candles, kerosene, and coal were used. The home had a cellar and water was retrieved from a well. Mail was delivered by rural route and they "had a cat named Blacky."

Mildred was the fourth child born and Myrtle was the youngest of the seven children. As children, their major chore, among others, was doing the dishes. Their mother did the cooking and ironing and she taught them to sew, crochet, knit, and embroider. Mildred learned to drive a car from a neighborhood boy and her husband, Randall Moon, taught her to cook. Mildred and Myrtle's father, Edward Batdorf, was a miner and Mildred worked to help contribute to the family income. She was fourteen years old when she secured her first job. The family had a garden and they "dug the ground and got it ready to plant. They grew potatoes, lettuce, celery, onions, tomatoes, peppers, cabbage and a lot more." They had cherry and peach trees. Their mother did canning and raised chickens and the family often ate beef, pork, and chicken. Her parents and siblings did all the work, hiring no one to help with the house, garden, or animals. "Saturday was the day that you got a rest for the weekend and Sunday we got ready for church." The family attended a small church in Loyalton. For Christmas they would wake up early to see the tree and they received clothes as gifts. On July Fourth, "my brother had a birthday and we had games that we played." In general, however, sibling's birthdays were just another day. For her birthday, Mildred received clothes made by her mother.

The family did not entertain often but they did go to family picnics. Mildred kept in touch with distant family and visited relatives often. In the summer, "we sat under a nice shade tree to keep cool" and in the winter kept warm with long johns. Mildred recalls one extreme winter storm when the snow reached up over the fences. For recreation, the children played jump rope, ball and cards. Mildred's best friend was Hilda Buffington and they often played games for fun. Mildred did not learn to swim and the family never went on vacation.

Growing up, there was no place to shop so the family ordered items from "men who came around and the next day he came with it." They never went to the city to shop but there was a small country store. Lykens was the largest town nearby and Mildred used to take the train to visit her grandmother in Elizabethville. My father "got a car when I was ten years old. It was a Ford model T." Mildred attended a little red one-room schoolhouse in Big Run. It was only two houses away and she usually walked to school alone. Mildred was closest to her mother and she admired her father most. When young, Mildred "hoped to be a good housekeeper." Her family supported and encouraged her and they influenced her and helped her develop skills. When asked if she would choose the same career path, she said, "No. I would choose for a better life." "I met my husband in Lykens. I was engaged on Easter and married on October 1, 1926." Mildred was married in Hagerstown to her husband, a dentist, and her children were born in Pennsylvania.

They likely did not have electricity for the first twenty-five years of their marriage, because as late as 1936, 75 percent of Pennsylvania farms were not electrified. So they used candles and lanterns for nighttime light, heated with coal, and fetched water from a well. The family kept a garden—really a small truck farm—growing potatoes, lettuce, celery, onions, tomatoes, peppers, and cabbages, cherry and peach trees, and raising chickens, cows, and hogs. The children were expected to help with chores, and by the age of fourteen or so, they were getting their first jobs and contributing to the family's expenses. Myrtle, the direct ancestor of the Thompson line, grew up and went to school as Big Run, which was in Washington Township.

CHAPTER 2

THOMAS EDWARD BATDORF
&
MARY LOUISE PETERS

THOMAS EDWARD BATDORF & MARY LOUISE PETERS

When Thomas Batdorf, named for his uncle Thomas Batdorf, was born to Peter Batdorf and Elizabeth Welker Batdorf in the Lykens/Big Run area of Dauphin County, Pennsylvania, in 1851, the United States of America was only seventy-five years old and Dauphin County, established in 1785, was only sixty-five years old.

Travel was by stagecoach, Conestoga wagon, canal, and ferry. Roads were dirt and, in the spring, nearly impassable mud, including the main road that connected Millersburg, Big Run, Lykens, and Elizabethville, and is Route 209 today.

The anthracite coal industry, which would dominate the economy in later years, was in its infancy in 1851, the coal having been discovered in 1825 and first shipped out of the area in 1834 to Millersburg by the Lykens Valley Railroad and Coal Company. At Millersburg, it was loaded on a Susquehanna River pole boat ferry. The railroad, which used horse power on a flat strip rail, was the fourth in the United States and the first in Dauphin County. Derailments were frequent and the 16-mile trip could take two days. Shipments stopped in 1845 when the railroad broke down until 1848 when the Wiconisco Canal was built and the railroad was improved with a T-rail. The coal was shipped as bulk ore until 1848 when the first coal breaker was built in Lykens.

With the coal industry just emerging in 1851 when Thomas was born, Dauphin County was virtually all rural and the economy depended on farming, hunting, fishing, and logging. Though much of the forests had been clear-cut for farms, buildings, heat, and lumber, perhaps 60 percent was still deeply wooded and home to pheasants, turkeys, deer, bear, and possibly even wolves and elk, though they were declining in Pennsylvania. The streams and lakes teemed with shad, salmon, and perch.

By December 6, 1874, when Thomas married Mary Peters, much had changed. Thousands more acres had been clear-cut, roads improved, and passenger train service established. Berrysburg, Elizabethville, and Lykens were officially incorporated as boroughs.

As Thomas had been, Mary was born in Dauphin County. Her father was Samuel Peters, who had been born in Union County, and she was named after her mother, Mary Swartz, who had been born in Mifflin, a township in Juniata County, the next county to the northeast of Dauphin County. Mary was the last of Samuel and Mary's seven children. Preceding her were John, Emma, Jonathan, Matthew, Matilda (known as Tillie), and Jane.

Though Pennsylvania's 1790 state constitution had mandated free public primary education, few children in the Lykens/Elizabethville area went to school beyond the equivalent of seventh grade. Note that Mary was only sixteen when she married Thomas. Thomas also came from a large family, being the tenth of eleven children of Peter and Mary Louise. Thomas's older siblings were Esther, Jonas, Elizabeth, Susan, John, Sarah, Peter, Anna, and Rebecca, and he was followed by his sister Louisa.

After Thomas and Mary married, they settled in Elizabethville, where it is likely he was working in the mines, as the 1880 census shows his occupation as a laborer and the 1890 census shows him working as a miner. "Miner" was not a general term for mine workers, but rather a specific job that required certification. The 1910 census shows him as a retired laborer.

The 1870 census shows that four years before he married he was a blacksmith apprentice in Berrysburg to Henry Wise, twenty-four, who had a wife, Sarah, and a one-year old son, Charles. Thomas was a religious man. He was baptized in the German Reformed St. Peters (Hoffman's) Church in Lykens and buried St. Johns Evangelical Lutheran (Oakdale) Cemetery in Loyalton when he died in 1916.

It is known that at least twice he attended the Pennsylvania Evangelical Conference in Berrysburg. In 1904 he attended with his wife and daughter Mary Ellen. In 1906 he attended with his wife, son Adam and daughter Frances.

Thomas died at the age of sixty-five of heart and kidney disease. Mary survived Thomas by eight years, dying in 1924 of a cerebral hemorrhage. Mary Louisa Peters was buried on August 6, 1924, in St. Johns (Oakdale) Cemetery, Loyalton, from the Buffington Funeral Home. Before she married Thomas, she was counted in the census in 1860 and 1870 with her family in Mifflin and Washington Townships, Dauphin County. In 1880, 1890, 1900, and 1910 she was counted in Washington Township and Elizabethville with her husband. After his death, and four years before her death, she was counted in the census in 1920, still in Elizabethville, working as a housekeeper. Thomas and his siblings lived through famous historical events, including the violent United Mine Workers Strike of 1902 (the only strike in which a sitting president, Theodore Roosevelt, intervened) and the Civil War.

Elizabethville was an important rail center during the Civil War. Men from the surrounding towns boarded trains there for Harrisburg to be mustered into the army. Among them was John Batdorf. Thomas, perhaps inspired by his older brother, though he was only fourteen in 1865 the last year of the war, lied about his age and enlisted. Unlike the five-foot-tall woman he would one day marry, Thomas was tall for his age, close to six feet. It was easy for the enlistment officers to believe he was eighteen, which was the age of enlistment. The Army did not require proof of age. They simply accepted.

While Thomas Batdorf, a man of family faith and country, and Mary Peters came from large families, their families were modest compared to the family they would create. They were the parents of seventeen children, born between the years of 1875 and 1899, a large family even by eighteenth century standards. Five of their children died in childhood, of those that lived into adulthood, their seventh child, James, is the direct ancestor of the Thompson line.

CHAPTER 3

JOHN HENRY WERT
&
ADELINE ROW

JOHN HENRY WERT & ADELINE ROW

John H. Wert was born in Dalmatia, Northumberland County, Pennsylvania, in 1855, the third of the eventual ten children of David M. Wert and Catherine Shoop. David's father was Jacob Wert. His mother was Sarah Faber. David was born on April 1, 1829, in Powell's Valley, Dauphin County. He was a farm laborer. John's mother, Catherine, was the daughter of John Shoop and Sarah Wertz. Catherine was born on February 24, 1830, in Northumberland County.

John and older siblings Elizabeth and Anna were born in Northumberland County. His younger siblings, Mary, Melinda, Amelia, Daniel, and Isaac, were born after the family moved to adjacent Dauphin County, which was more prosperous than Northumberland.

John was working as a blacksmith in Washington Township, Dauphin County, when he met his wife, Adeline Row. Adeline was born in Dauphin County near Lykens borough on January 2, 1860. Her father was Daniel Row and her mother was Susan Frantz. Daniel was the son of John William Rowe and Barbara Rudy. He was born on July 10, 1813, in Dauphin County. Susan Frantz was born March 23, 1819, in Dauphin County. She was the daughter of Adam Frantz and Susan Gieseman.

Adeline was the youngest of seven siblings, following Sarah, Angelina, Adam, Susan, Amelia, and Leah. By 1870, the family had broken up. Adeline was living with her aunt, Susan Ely. Her father, Daniel, died on July 31, 1871, when Adeline was eleven.

John and Adeline married in 1878. She was eighteen, he was twenty-three. They wed in the "Church of the Hill," St. John's Lutheran Church. Built of stone on a hill overlooking the Lykens Valley in 1872, it replaced a log church built in 1802. The parish roots dated back to 1773 when the Reverend J. Enderline, a pioneer missionary, came to Lykens Valley.

John and Adeline settled in Washington Township, Dauphin County. By 1900, John had given up blacksmithing. The trade was in decline with the rise of factories, the development of the casting process, and less demand for horses in agriculture and transport. He became a freelance day laborer. That meant he was not on regular payroll of a farm or mine, but hired himself out on a daily basis where labor was needed. Since work was not steady, he needed help supporting his family. Adeline helped out running a farm on their property in Washington Township in the 1910s.

In 1879 they had a daughter, Caroline Wert. They eventually had five more children. Harriet was born in 1881. Another child, about whom little is known, was born in 1883. Florence was born on March 6, 1886. Beulah was born on New Year's Eve in 1889. Finally, Margaret was born in 1904.

John was a big man for the day at six-foot and a hard and willing worker. He coveted a union job with one of the coal companies. But in May 1902, United Mine Workers president John Mitchell organized an anthracite workers strike. In November of that year, U.S. President Teddy Roosevelt, fearing a shortage of coal for the winter, threatened to send in federal troops to take over the mines. Only then did the sides agree to end the strike.

After the strike, the coal companies refused to let replacement workers go and over half the men who went on strike in Lykens Valley were not called back. That didn't help John. But the growth of the anthracite industry did help. The growth of the coal industry, and the Dauphin economy, was jumped-started by the Civil War. John and Adeline's home in Washington Township was only 80 miles from the Mason-Dixon Line and 60 miles from Gettysburg. Thus, Dauphin County, as a breadbasket and coal producer, was important to the Union. Pennsylvania supplied 80 percent of the Union Army's iron, all of its anthracite coal, and much of its textiles and food, with Dauphin a large contributor.

After the Civil War an enormous demand for anthracite and technological advances in mining during the industrial revolution fueled exponential growth in the industry. America's entry into World War I created even more demand. The anthracite industry peaked in 1917, when one hundred eighty thousand workers harvested one hundred million tons of coal throughout the anthracite region of Eastern Pennsylvania. John was one of those workers. He was hired by the Susquehanna Colliery in Lykens in the 1910s. This is evident because in the 1910 census he was a "day laborer" and in 1920 he was a "laborer–coal mine." John was still working for the Susquehanna Colliery in 1922, when a modern electric plant was built to provide electricity to all the local collieries. The $2 million plant burned "coal dirt," or culm, the by-product of coal processing.

John was 67 and still working for Susquehanna in October of 1924, when he was crushed by rolling logs while cutting timber for mine tunnels. He was taken to the Harrisburg Hospital where he died. Cause of death was a hemorrhage and shock from fractured ribs and other injuries. He outlived Adeline by three years. She was fifty-nine when she died of natural causes in 1921. John and Adeline were waked at the Buffington Funeral Home in Elizabethville and buried in St. John's Cemetery.

Though mine work was dangerous and workers were paid less than their value, the pay for a union mine worker in the 1910s and early 20s was better than the average worker's salary in other industries. In the decades before their deaths, John and Adeline may have had some extra income from his job and her farm. Their daughter Beulah, who was ten in

1900, lived with them. As they lived in rural Washington Township they likely had fun taking Beulah to family and church picnics, fairs, moving pictures, and baseball games in the boroughs around the township. They lived on State Road, which was macadam by the 1910s and provided easy access to Elizabethville and Lykens.

In these towns, Adeline could shop at general merchandise and confectionary stores. At the market she could find butter at twenty cents per pound, eggs at eighteen cents per dozen, and dressed chickens at ten cents per pound. As she ran a small farm she may have been a buyer or seller. John might visit taverns, billiard halls, and cigar stores. If they needed to visit the state capital, Harrisburg, twenty miles to the south, they could leave from the train station in Elizabethville—an important troop depot in the Civil War. Built in 1875, the station is still standing today. Also in the towns in the 1880s and 1890s banks were established, rudimentary telephone service began, water companies were organized, and fire departments were formed. Electric lights and moving pictures came in 1909, though these conveniences arrived much later in the townships. They must have seemed like amazing technologies to John and Adeline, who had grown up before electricity, plumbing, and paved roads.

As they traveled among the towns, John and Adeline may have been even more amazed to see a flying machine in the sky. In April of 1913, Walter Johnson of New York flew from Millersburg to Wisconisco in 13 minutes.

Fair going was a pastime. The biggest was seven miles from Lykens in Gratz, which boasted a first-class horse track. At baseball games, John and Adeline might well have watched family members play in the Twin County League. It is known that in 1921, the center fielder, named Wert, set a league record for stolen bases, and a player named Row batted .326 and was third in the league in runs. John and Adeline had at least enough schooling to be literate. Reading newspapers was a popular pastime. The towns all had local papers at one time or another and people also read the Harrisburg Patriot, which chronicled daily life in its town columns. Folks might read that "a coat of paint greatly improved Adam Row's house in Lykens" or "Carrie Wert of Millersburg visited her parents, John, and wife for several days." "Carrie" was a nickname for daughter Caroline.

In addition to his fierce work ethic, John was a devoted family man. In 1920, a grandson, John Schoffer, age seven, lived with him and Adeline. John and Adeline's youngest daughter, Beulah, is the direct ancestor of the Thompson line. After she married James "Edward" Batdorf, they and her parents lived on adjacent farms at 46 and 47 State Road in Washington Township.

CHAPTER 4

PETER BATDORF
&
ELIZABETH WELKER

PETER BATDORF & ELIZABETH WELKER

In a sense, Peter Batdorf and his wife, Elizabeth Welker, were war babies. She was born on November 23 in 1812, four months after America declared war on Great Britain beginning the War of 1812. He was born January 20, 1814, eleven months before the treaty was signed ending the war. The war must have seemed distant to their families—the only Pennsylvania battle was at Lake Erie. News of the battle probably took a month to reach Dauphin County, Pennsylvania.

Peter and Elizabeth were born in Lykens Township, Dauphin County, at a time when America was less than forty years old. She was named for her mother, Maria "Elizabeth" Messerschmidt, he for his father, Jacob "Peter" Batdorf. Lykens is named for Andrew Lycans. He settled on a tract of about two hundred acres on the Whiconescong Creek in 1755, near what is now Loyalton Borough. He cleared land and built houses for his family and a small group of subsequent settlers. Lycans lived in relative peace for no more than a year.

Then in 1756, during the French and Indian War, Lycans was driven from his home and eventually died while retreating from Indians. The Indians were allied with the French against the British and the colonists. The hostilities with the Indians ended in 1764, after which Lycan's widow returned to the old home.

By 1810, when Peter was born, the Indians had been driven to the west. Peter was the first of nine children of Jacob Peter Batdorf and Maria Catherine Steiner. Sarah, John, Catherine, Thomas, Jonathan, Daniel, Jacob, and Elizabeth were Peter's young siblings. Peter's father, Jacob, was born in 1793. His mother, Maria, was born in 1792. Though it's not known if Jacob was born in Dauphin County, it is certain that he lived and died there. Maria was born in adjacent Berks County. How she migrated to the Lykens area of Dauphin County isn't clear. It may have been with her family or after she married Jacob. In either case, it may have been no more than ten to fifteen miles.

Elizabeth Welker was the fourth child of John Welker and Maria Elizabeth Messerschmidt, both natives of Dauphin County. John was born in 1783, Maria Elizabeth in 1780. Elizabeth followed siblings George, Rachel, and a daughter whose name is not known. Her younger siblings were William, David, Anna, Sarah, and Joseph.

Peter was nineteen and Elizabeth was twenty-one when they were married in 1831, most likely in St. Peter's Reformed Church in nearby Loyalton. Also known as the Hoffman Church, it was erected about 1771 by Anthony Hautzon on land donated by the Hoffman family, early settlers in Lykens Township. Peter was baptized there and both he and Elizabeth were buried there. They both died in Dauphin County—she in 1868, he in 1880.

In each census during their lifetimes, Peter and Elizabeth were counted in Lykens Township (not to be confused with Lykens Borough, which was settled within the township in 1832, but not incorporated until 1871). The township was incorporated in 1810 covering fifty square miles in northern Dauphin County. In 1839, it was divided to form Wiconisco Township. In the pre-Civil War nineteenth century, Lykens Township was a remote area of scattered farms in a stunning green valley teeming with wildlife and fishing creeks. The population density was less ten per square mile.

Peter and Elizabeth would live out their lives where they were born. It's not likely they ever traveled more than ten to twenty miles from their home. There was nothing unusual about that. Travel was by wagon over dirt roads that were little more than widened and packed Indian trails. Moving a large family would have been daunting. Besides where would Peter and Elizabeth go, and to do what?

The American economy took off after the War of 1812. The steam engine, patented in 1783 by James Watt, came into widespread use in factories and mills, especially in New England and major cities in the East. But the Industrial Revolution was slow in coming to remote and sparsely populated rural areas like the Lykens Valley. There were no factories in the Dauphin County in the early decades of the nineteenth century. The first known stationary steam engine, as opposed to those used in trains and the ferries at Millersburg and Harrisburg, was brought to Lykens in 1830, when the Lycans settlement consisted of no more than thirty log homes.

Because of these conditions, the Lykens Valley economy was only marginally monetary-based before the Civil War. Self-sufficiency and barter drove the citizens' lives. Peter was self-sufficient as a Yeoman. Though "Yeoman" is commonly thought of as a low naval rank in nineteenth-century America, it also meant a family farmer who owned a small plot of land. Elizabeth kept house and probably made clothes to be handed down for their eleven children, at least in the early years of their marriage. While the first store was opened in the Lykens settlement in 1832, it wasn't until after the Civil War that mercantiles offered factory-made clothes affordable to average folks like the Batdorfs.

Esther was the first born of Peter and Elizabeth's children, followed by Jonas, Elizabeth, Susan, John, Sarah, Peter, Anna, Rebecca, Thomas, and Louisa. The family was closer to average than large for the time period.

Peter was probably a Yeoman for the first a decade or so of their marriage. In the 1840s, as Dauphin became more connected by canals and rail, he may have farmed cash crops such as wheat. In 1825, coal was discovered on Short Mountain overlooking Lykens Valley. This was no ordinary coal, but anthracite of the first order—89 percent carbon. It was shipped crudely by wagon until 1832, when the Lykens Valley Railroad and Coal Company was created by an act of the legislature. The railroad created a need for coal mining laborers that grew exponentially when local breakers were built, the first in Dauphin County in 1848 in Lykens.

Steam engines would come into widespread use in Dauphin with the rise of the coal industry. They were used to drive pumps, fans and conveyers before the collieries made electricity. The breakers increased coal production for the Civil War effort, the growth of factories, and large-scale iron forges. The need for laborers could be met only one way—immigration. They came from Scotland, Ireland, Germany, and other parts of Europe, doubling the population of Dauphin County in the mid-nineteenth century. Though the anthracite mines were notorious for accidents and worker exploitation, the coal greatly enhanced the Dauphin economy and sped technological advances.

Peter entered his fifties during the Civil War. He was too old to be drafted, but took advantage of the ancillary jobs created by burgeoning coal industry and the war.

Peter worked as a carpenter from 1850 to 1870. He may have been building log homes and churches for immigrant families. He might also have helped build furniture, canal locks, or railroads ties.

After Elizabeth died in 1868, Peter married Magdalena "Mollie" Lettich. His marriage to Mollie, and his advancing age, may have prompted Peter to go back to farming. He may have been aided by organizations of farmers, such as the Grange, that fought to improve the conditions for yeomen. The Pennsylvania Grange was organized in v.

When Peter and Mollie married they were beyond childbearing years, so they did not affect the Thompson line. Peter and Elizabeth's second youngest, Thomas, is the direct line.

CHAPTER 5

SAMUEL PETERS
&
MARY ANN SWARTZ

SAMUEL PETERS & MARY LOUISE SWARTZ

How remote was Union County, Pennsylvania, when Samuel Peters was born there in 1821? In 1821, the Pennsylvania Canal system hadn't yet reached Union. A railroad connection was forty-plus years away. Fewer than fifty years earlier, the area was on the frontier of European settlement. The County had been formed in 1813 when land west of the Susquehanna River was separated from Northumberland County. It was divided into Union and Snyder counties in 1855. Samuel was the first born of five children of John and Anna Maria Peters. Anna's maiden name is unknown. Samuel was followed by brothers, Andrew, Jonathan, Elias, and a sister, Matilda.

Samuel's father, John, was born in New Jersey in 1795. It's not known exactly when he migrated to Union County, nor when he married Anna—whom he met in Union—though it is very likely he migrated just a year or so before Samuel was born in 1821 and settled in Buffalo Township. As with most of the early settlers of Union County, John likely migrated there for work or to acquire land, which was being allotted by application.

When Samuel grew up he did not go to school, as there weren't any in the Buffalo area. In 1834, the state legislature passed a bill mandating counties to create common, or public, schools. Afraid of the cost, most of which had to be met at the local level, Union County created a committee of fifteen men to draft a resolution objecting to the bill. It passed in Union Township 154–12 in 1840. Countywide the vote was 1,620 to 267.

As soon as Samuel was old enough—eight or so—he most likely worked for his father on the family's subsistence farm. When he was thirteen in 1834, a "black" frost hit the Buffalo Valley on May 31 and June 1. It was so cold that whole orchards of apples, pears, and cherries were killed. Bears looking for food came down from the mountains to feed on green corn and scores were killed by farmers. Birds survived and thrived, as caterpillars were prodigious.

Samuel went out on his own when he married Mary Ann Swartz, who had been born in nearby Juniata County in 1821. Juniata County was formed on March 2, 1831, from parts of Mifflin County. Nothing is known about Mary Ann's mother. All that is known about her family is that her father, John Swartz, was a native Pennsylvanian, born about 1794, and that she had a brother, John.

Samuel and Mary Ann were married somewhere between 1840 and 1843, when both were in their early twenties. They may have been married at the Lutheran and Reformed Church that was dedicated in Buffalo Township in 1839. We can deduce when they married because, in the 1840 census, Samuel was living with his mother and Mary Ann was living with her father in Union Township, Union County. Then in 1850, they were counted together in the census in Union County with three children; the oldest, John, was six. They had six more children: Emma, Jonathan, Matthew, Matilda, and twins Jane and Mary Louisa, who were born in 1858.

There were 242 families in Union Township in 1850 and a total population of 1,436. Nearly every family had its own home. There were 235 dwellings in the township. There was one merchant and two clerks at the township's only mercantile. There was one inn and one physician. Three men were employed as "limeburners." There were a smattering of blacksmiths and wheelwrights, but eighty-five percent of the men worked as farmers or laborers, Samuel among them. In the mid-nineteenth century, there was plenty of labor to be done in Central Pennsylvania. Forested land had to be cleared for the building of settlements, roads, rail beds, gristmills, dams, and canals. Much of the money for such projects came from lotteries. The Union Canal lottery was conducted in 1826. Sometime in the 1850s Samuel and Mary Ann moved east to Mifflin Township in Dauphin County, where Peters was a common surname. Peters Mountain runs for thirty miles in central Dauphin County.

Dauphin was further east and closer to the roads and rail lines to Philadelphia, York, and Harrisburg than Union. Dauphin had been settled earlier and was more progressive, more populated, more developed and richer than Union. For example, Dauphin had a good school system, with nine one-room schoolhouses, as early as 1830. It is likely Samuel and Mary moved for better work opportunities for Samuel, but the existence of good schools may also have been a lure. Perhaps Mary, who could not read and write, wanted better for her children. It is known that Jonathan and Tillie, at least, went to school in Dauphin.

In 1860, Samuel was still working as a laborer at a time when there was even more work available. The anthracite coal industry was increasing in Dauphin County. Though it is believed Samuel never worked directly for a coal company, the industry created peripheral work. Better road and railroads were needed for the industry. Homes, churches, and schools were needed in the boroughs for the immigrant mineworkers. Samuel could have worked as a laborer for farmers, road builders, carpenters, or stonemasons. The farmers also benefited from the better roads and railroads as they moved from subsistence farming to the commercial farming of food for cities. Philadelphia was having a growth spurt of its own, and could not feed itself. Dauphin County provided commercial quantities of wheat, corn, linseed oil, rye, and whiskey. The Civil War build-up—which began when Lincoln was reelected President in November—and the war itself also increased economic activity and work.

During the war, Samuel went to Perry County, a small county that bordered Dauphin at the Susquehanna north of Harrisburg in the Millersburg area. It's not known what Samuel was doing in Perry County. Had he gone there to work? Had he and Mary split? What is known is that he died there in about 1865 and that before he left Dauphin he and Mary had one last child, Mary Louisa. Perry wasn't far from Samuel's home in Dauphin by rail or from where he grew up in Union by ferry. He was only 44 and may have been in Perry working or he may have been ill and staying with relatives. He was buried in Perry County.

Mary Ann outlived Samuel by thirty-two years. After his death she moved to the Lykens area and worked as a housekeeper. In the 1880s she retired and moved in with her daughter, Jane, and her husband Alfred Row in Washington Township, Dauphin County. She was seventy-five when she died in 1897 of heart disease. She was buried in St. Johns Oakdale Cemetery, Loyalton. Samuel and May left a legacy—family. Their "caboose" Mary, one of the twins they had in their late thirties, turned out to be the direct line to the Thompson family. Mary married Thomas Batdorf.

CHAPTER 6

DAVID M. WERT
&
CATHERINE SHOOP

DAVID M. WERT & CATHERINE SHOOP

David Wert was the son of parents who bucked the odds. His father, Jacob Wert, and mother, Sarah Faber, both native Pennsylvanians, were born in 1804 and 1807, respectively, when the average life expectancy was forty-five years. Sarah, the daughter of John Faber and Maria Rudy, lived to ninety-five. Jacob, the son of John Wirth and Anna Miller, lived to eighty-four. Because records were hand-written in the early eighteenth century, different spellings of last names were not unusual.

Though not as long-lived as his parents, David did live to seventy-one, a longer-than-average lifespan in the nineteenth century. During his life, David worked as a laborer, was married twice, and fathered fourteen children. But it was one of the ten children he had with his first wife, Catherine Shoop, who is of most interest here.

David was born in Powells Valley, Dauphin County, Pennsylvania, on April 1, 1829. David was the oldest of nine siblings, followed by Elizabeth, Catherine, Sarah, John, Adam, Peter, Matthew, and Martha. He died two years before his mother on December 9, 1900, in Dayton, Dauphin County, Pennsylvania, of lung congestion. He was buried from the Calvary United Methodist, or Union, Church in Wiconisco, Dauphin County. Wiconisco was laid out in 1848. The church was erected in 1854.

David married Catherine Shoop about 1849 in Dauphin County. He was twenty and she was nineteen. Catherine was the daughter of John Shoop and Sarah Wertz. Catherine was born on February 24, 1830, in Northumberland County, which borders Dauphin to the north. Catherine was baptized on March 6, 1830, in the Stone Valley Reformed Lutheran Church, also known as Zion Church, in Northumberland County. The church was established in the 1770s. She was the second oldest of four girls. Her older sister was Anna Shoop and her younger sisters were Anna Maria, Elizabeth, and Salome, or Sarah.

David and Catherine probably met at a church function or through relatives. In any case, they didn't live far apart. Catherine was counted in the census in 1830 and 1840 with her father in Lower Mahanoy, Northumberland County, which was about ten to fifteen miles from Halifax, Dauphin County, where David was counted in the census in 1830 and 1840 with his family.

After they married, David and Catherine moved to Upper Paxton, Dauphin County, which was right between their families' homes in Halifax and Lower Mahanoy. They most likely moved for work, though being equidistant from their families was a plus. Upper Paxton was bordered by Mahantango Mountain to the north, Berry Mountain to the south, and the Susquehanna River to the west. The nearest town, Millersburg, was an important ferry town on the river. The area was rich with timber, streams, and wildlife. As a laborer, David might have worked building roads, laying rail, and digging canals, though more likely as a farmer. They lived in Upper Paxton in the early 1850s, but in the late 1850s, they moved to her home area of Lower Mahanoy, Northumberland County. David was not drafted during the Civil War—though he was well within age (being thirty in 1860), he was married with four children under age six, and that may have been a factor.

Perhaps prompted by Catherine's father's death in 1859, David and Catherine moved again to the Lykens area of Washington Township in Dauphin County, where they were counted in the census of 1870. By then they had all of their ten children: Elizabeth, Anna, John Henry, Mary, Melinda, Martha, Catherine, Amelia, Daniel, and Isaac. David likely worked as a farm laborer for one of their neighbors. There was plenty of work—the area was booming economically with the growth of the anthracite coal industry. Immigrants were moving to the area to work the mines and they had to be fed, clothed, and housed. Also, commercial farming was growing as families moved into the cities following the Civil War, where they were more likely to buy food than to grow it. This was the beginning of a trend that would accelerate with the Industrial Revolution.

Recreation in the Dauphin area in the eighteenth century revolved round family, church, neighborhoods, organizations such as the Grange, and work. Families gathered at holidays, churches held socials, neighbors got together to build barns and Granges, and workplaces threw picnics with games for kids and adults.

Catherine died on June 8, 1872. She was buried from St. Peters Reformed Lutheran Church, also known as the Hoffman Church, in Loyalton, Dauphin County, near Lykens. After Catherine's death, David moved by himself to Union Township, Berks County, where he was counted in the 1880 census as a boarder of Winfred Allison, a widower with three young children.

Son John, then fifteen, went to live with Jacob and Elizabeth Seiler in Jackson Township, Northumberland County. His sisters Martha and Catherine (also known as Kate), lived with families in the Lykens area as maids or servants. By 1900, David and second wife, Elizabeth Bellis, moved back to Washington Township,

Dauphin County.

The many place names mentioned above might leave the impression that the families traveled widely in the eighteenth century, but they didn't. Powells Valley, Stone Valley, Upper Paxton, Lower Mahanoy, Lykens, Washington Township, Jackson Township, Wiconisco, Halifax, and the counties of Dauphin, Northumberland, and Union are all within five to twenty-five miles of each other and the larger Lykens Valley area.

The climate was moderate with plenty of rain. All the areas had similar landscapes of lush valleys and rolling mountains of hardwood trees—such as oak, chestnut, hickory, and beech—and softer woods like white pine. But these landscapes changed during David's lifetime. When Europeans first explored the area, trees covered more than 90 percent of Dauphin County's 400,000 acres. But steel plows and axles allowed European settlers to quickly clear large areas of forest for subsistence farming. There were probably one thousand subsistence farms in Dauphin County by 1860. In the later part of the century, clear-cutting to lay out towns and facilitate mining destroyed large swaths of forest. By the 1850s, Pennsylvania was the nation's largest supplier of lumber and other wood products such as wood alcohol and tannic acid from hemlock, used to process hides. By 1900, the year David died, Dauphin had lost more than 60 percent of its forests. Rain washed soil from the clear-cut areas into streams, and forest fires burned through the dead stumps, dry branches, scrub brush, and saplings, ruining fish and wildlife habitat.

The Europeans saw the forests as dollar signs and as an impediment to development. Little attention was paid to the negative effects of clear-cutting until the Pennsylvania Commission of Forestry was founded in 1901. After World War I, many rural Pennsylvanians moved into the cities and abandoned farms were reforested.

David Wert was not one of those who moved to a city, though by 1890s—when he moved to Lykens—it was a well-developed area due to the economic spillover of the anthracite industry. David was still working as a laborer right up until his death in 1900. It was David's son John Henry who was the direct ancestor of the Thompson line. John was working as a blacksmith in Washington Township when he met his wife, Adeline Row. Later he became a union miner at the Susquehanna colliery in Lykens.

CHAPTER 7

DANIEL ROW
&
SUSAN FRANTZ

DANIEL ROW & SUSAN FRANTZ

Daniel Row was born on July 10, 1813, in Dauphin County, Pennsylvania. Though the War of 1812 was being fought at the time, it had no impact in Dauphin County. The only Pennsylvania Battle was on Lake Erie, where Captain Perry defeated the British two months after Daniel was born.

Daniel was the third child of Barbara Rudy and John William Rowe. His older siblings were Wendell and Jacob. His younger siblings were Susan, John, Elizabeth, Sarah, and Joseph. Daniel lived to age fifty-eight. He died on July 31, 1871, in Dauphin County. Though that was a fairly long life for the time, he was outlived by both his parents. His father, John, was born in June 1785 in Strasburg, Lancaster County, Pennsylvania, and lived to age ninety-two, dying in 1877 in Berrysburg, Dauphin County. Daniel's mother, Barbara, was born in April 1796 also in Strasburg. She died at age eighty-five on December 15, 1881, also in Berrysburg, Dauphin County.

Daniel's parents migrated to Dauphin from Strasburg soon after they married, probably around 1810. The Strasburg-Lancaster area was more developed than Dauphin County, which was an area of forests pockmarked by subsistence farms. It is likely Daniel and Susan moved for the adventure—a desire to strike out on their own and for land—perhaps urged on by relatives who were already in Dauphin. It wasn't an easy journey. Though only 75 miles, the journey likely took a week to ten days by Conestoga wagon, stagecoach, or on foot or horseback. They may have been in a caravan of settlers traveling on dirt roads that were little more than widened Indian trails passing through the Blue, Second, and Peters Mountains. In any case, when Daniel was born, they were in Dauphin in the Halifax area. John was working as a farm laborer.

Daniel married Susan Frantz, a native of Dauphin County, in the late 1830s when she was in her late teens and he was twenty-five. This is evident because both were living with their parents in 1830 and they were together in 1840. Susan Frantz was born March 23, 1819. She was named for her mother, Susan Giesemen, who was born in 1787 in Tulpehocken, Berks County. Her father, Adam Frantz, was born in 1780 in Lykens, Dauphin County. She was the third youngest of their eight children. Her older siblings were William, Jacob, Catherine, John, and Christina and her younger siblings were Sarah and Samuel.

Unlike her husband's parents, Susan's parents died young. Her father was in his forties when died between 1825 and 1830 in Dauphin County. Her mother was forty-nine when she died in 1826. It was a fate that would also befall Susan. She died in 1861 at age forty-two, with four young girls—Susan, Amelia, Leah, and Adeline—still living at home. The girls were four of the seven children of Daniel and Susan. Their older siblings were Sarah, Angeline, and Adam, the lone son.

After Susan's death, the family scattered. In 1870, Daniel—who would die within a year—was living with Jacob Zerber in Berrysburg and still working as a laborer. Daughter Susan was eighteen and working as a cook in a boarding home near Berrysburg. Amelia was living with David Matter, a successful farmer in Washington Township with a farm valued at $11,500 (the equivalent of $500,000 today). Leah was living with John Lebo, a butcher in Lykens. Adeline was just three doors away living with her aunt Susan Ely and attending school.

Daniel never attended school and was illiterate, not an unusual circumstance for men of his generation who worked farms in rural Pennsylvania. But Daniel had a descendant who was different. Daniel's nephew, Jonas Row, was his brother Jacob's son. Jonas was one of the most interesting members of the extended family. Jonas was a farmer, yes, but he attended school. Over the years, he was active in politics and was a supervisor of roads, a tax collector, and a justice of the peace. He was also a butcher and a merchant. Somehow he found time to be a deacon, trustee, and Sunday-school superintendent and teacher in the Lutheran Church.

During the Civil War in 1863, Jonas enlisted in the Union Army at Harrisburg. Assigned to the One Hundred and Twenty-seventh Regiment, Pennsylvania volunteers, under Colonel Jennings and Captain Bell, he participated in the battle of Gettysburg and was wounded in the knee. He was discharged after only three months' service. Though the wound left him lame him for life, it didn't stop him from re-enlisting in the fall of 1863. With Company F, Sixteenth Pennsylvania, he was at Petersburg for five days, where bravery in action got him promoted to the rank of Orderly to General Gregg. Jonas was at the surrender of General Lee, and was mustered out of service in 1865.

After the war, he bought fifty-five acres and sunk $5,000 into developing a farm. He took a loss on that farm after using it as security for a loan for a friend. But again, he was not stopped from achieving his goals. He bought another eighty acres in Jefferson Township near Lykens and built a successful farm. Well-known and highly respected, he died in Schuylkill County at the age of eighty-two.

Daniel died in July 1871 of Bright's disease, a chronic inflammation of kidneys. For the first half of Daniel's life, the economy of the Lykens Valley area of Dauphin County was subsistence farming and the few peripheral businesses needed to support the farms, such as blacksmiths and limeburners, who burned limestone to create lime for fertilizer. There was very little commerce. Three things changed that in the second half of Daniel's life: the growth of the anthracite coal industry, the Civil War, and the emergence of the industrial revolution. Improved roads, the Pennsylvania canal system, and rail lines connected the area to the outside world. Timber, coal, and farm products became valuable commodities. Money replaced barter and banks were established in the towns such as Lykens, Berrysburg, and Elizabethville. Daniel was always counted as a nonspecific laborer in the census reports during his adult life. Though he wasn't a union miner or railroader, it's not hard to imagine him doing any or all of the necessary down-to-earth labor the modernization of Dauphin County required. There was plenty of work for a man with a strong back and a shovel.

Daniel was buried from the St. John's Lutheran Church in Berrysburg, Dauphin County, just as his wife, Susan, had been ten years earlier. Also known as the "Church of the Hill," it was the same church where Daniel was baptized in 1813. It was also the same church where generations of the extended family were baptized, married, and buried. The "Church of the Hill" had been built of stone on a hill overlooking the Lykens Valley in 1872, replacing a log church built in 1802. The parish roots dated back to 1773, when the Reverend J. Enderline, a pioneer missionary, came to Lykens Valley.

Daniel and Susan's youngest daughter, Adeline, was the direct line ancestor to the

Thompson family. Early life wasn't easy for Adeline. She lost her mother when she was one year old and her father when she was ten. Adeline grew up fast and started her adult life at age eighteen in 1878 when she married John H. Wert. He was twenty-three. Appropriately, they married in the "Church of the Hill," St. John's Lutheran Church, within sight of her parents' graves.

CHAPTER 8

BATDORF
AHNENTAFEL

ANCESTORS OF MYRTLE ADELINE BATDORF

Generation 1

1. **Myrtle Adeline Batdorf** (daughter of James "Edward" Batdorf and Beulah Irene Wert) was born on January 5, 1918 in Big Run, Dauphin County, Pennsylvania, USA[1, 2]. She died on May 8, 1983 in Polyclinic Hospital, Harrisburg, Dauphin County, Pennsylvania, USA[3, 4]. She married **Harper Bruce Thompson** (son of Abel Robert Thompson and Augusta "Gussie" Mae Hensel) on June 15, 1935 in St. Johns (Hill) Lutheran, Berrysburg, Dauphin County, Pennsylvania, USA[2, 5]. He was born on September 28, 1907 in Sheridan, Schuylkill County, Pennsylvania, USA[6, 7, 8]. He died on July 23, 1981 in Polyclinic Hospital, Harrisburg, Dauphin County, Pennsylvania, USA[7, 8].

Myrtle Adeline Batdorf was baptized on October 11, 1918 in Evangelical Lutheran Circuit, Lykens, Dauphin County, Pennsylvania, USA[5]. She was buried in 1983 (Lakeside Lutheran Church[3, 9]). She was buried on May 11, 1983 in Woodlawn Memorial Gardens, Harrisburg, Dauphin County, Pennsylvania, USA. Her cause of death was Cardiorespiratory arrest w/ASHD w/pacemaker[4]. She was counted in the census in 1920 in Washington, Dauphin County, Pennsylvania, USA[10]. She was counted in the census in 1930 in Lykens, Dauphin County, Pennsylvania, USA[11]. She was counted in the census in 1940 in Tower City, Schuylkill County, Pennsylvania, USA[12]. She was educated at School in 1930[13]. Her height was 5 ft. 9 in.. She had a medical condition of cardiac arrest due to arteriosclerosis, arthritis, cataracts, diabetes, heart disease, hypertension, obesity. She was employed as a Housewife in 1983[4]. Her estate was probated between May 10-19 1983 in Harrisburg, Dauphin County, Pennsylvania, USA[14]. She was affiliated with the Lutheran religion. She lived in Beaufort Farms, Camp Curtain, Estherton, Fort Hunter, Harrisburg, Hecktown, Lucknow, Rockville, Uptown, Windsor farms, all Dauphin County, Pennsylvania, USA in 1983[15]. She lived in 2660A Green St., Harrisburg, Dauphin County, Pennsylvania, USA in 1983[3, 4]. Her Social Security Number was 165-26-7303[4, 15]. She signed her will on March 30, 1979 in Harrisburg, Dauphin County, Pennsylvania, USA[14]. Funeral: 1983 in

Jesse H Geigle, 2100 Linglestown Rd.,Harrisburg, Dauphin County, Pennsylvania, USA[16] Political Party: in Democrat

Notes for Myrtle Adeline Batdorf:
Myrtle was named for her grandmother "Adeline" Row.

Funeral for Myrtle Thompson,
Pastor Gregory Harbaugh, John 11:1-43, May 1983
Myrtle Thompson's death came as a big surprise to me. I'm sure that was true for many of you--especially her family. I was called by Vaughn Miller on Monday morning. The family had asked if I would take care of the funeral services. I said I would and asked who died. 'Myrtle Thompson', he said. The name didn't ring a bell. I thought for a while. 'You took care of her husband's funeral.' Thompson. Harper. Myrtle. I was stunned. I sat down. I had visited her Friday and she was fine. We had a good talk. She had been thinking a lot about her mom, her sons and Harper, with .Mother's Day coming up and all. She shared some stories--and told me her doctor said she was fine but she wanted to lose some weight. She hugged me when I left with the bags she had kept for the Food Pantry. Then on Sunday, I saw Myrtle in church. I was stunned on Monday morning. I liked Myrtle. I will miss her. So will you. A sad Mother's Day for you--Beulah, Gerry, Gene and Bob--for your families, for friends. A sad day--period. We begin to think of the 'what ifs' or the 'might have beens.' I know I do. I think: I might have visited Myrtle more often, to talk. She worried a lot. I might have helped. You probably do the same. Perhaps you are somewhat angry--with yourself; with God for taking her; with Myrtle for leaving so suddenly--and on Mother's Day, no less. Martha was angry with Jesus when Lazarus died. They had called him when their brother became ill. But he had delayed, taken too long. Lazarus died. His friend Jesus--the healer and wonder-worker--had failed him. And Jesus wept. But Martha was angry. Listen to their dialog with some different tones: 'Jesus, where've you been? If you wouldn't have taken so long, Lazarus wouldn't have died. So, why don't you ask God to do something now.' Jesus replied, 'Martha, you know Lazarus will rise again.' 'Of course I know that--on the last day.' But I'm talking about now! Perhaps not. Perhaps Martha was soft and pious in her sorrow. She went out to meet him though. She was aggressive. Perhaps seeking. I suspect angry. And Jesus accepted the confrontation with

care and comfort and strength: 'I am the resurrection and the life; whoever believes in me will live and never die.' Yet Myrtle is dead. We know that. The story of her life for us has come to a sudden close. All we have left are the memories. Yet, a sudden unexpected death was just like Myrtle. I mean, it fits the story. The time I've known Myrtle she's been loving, but tough. Caring but straight forward and painfully honest. She said what she thought and meant it. I always knew where I stood with Myrtle. And she told me stories of how she handled I 'her boys' and how she always told Harper, "You let people use you too much." "I won't put up with that!" Fiercely independent and self-assertive. Even abrupt. But caring--sort of the 'thundering, velvet hand' of Dan Fogleberg's song. Myrtle loved her family deeply. And you loved her and remember her. So, we come together wondering, perhaps, 'where were you Lord?' Sad, angry, hurt. Yet, we recognize that all of us will die, all of our stories, our biographies will end. Lazarus died. But Jesus called him back 'that you may come to believe', he told his disciples. Jesus added a few chapters. And hanged the message. Like the disciples, we look at death as the last reality, the lost fight-of-life, the end. Even when we think in terms of the dead person's soul going to heaven, we have to face the reality that Myrtle is no longer with us--no more talking, or aughing or yelling or threats or love will come from Myrtle. We see death as the end of the story. But the story of Lazarus is a sign for us that the story is not over--'whoever believes in me will never die! That's the promise of Jesus--the one who died and who now lives. Lazarus would die again. Jesus is risen and returned to the Father--forever. I am the way, the truth and the life. No one comes to the Father except by me'. Risen. To give us hope--for life, for living. Yes, Myrtle is dead. But we are not. We remember her life, and we will tell stories about her, and we will live with hope that new chapters will yet be added by our Lord who brings life from death. We are alive--to go from here back to our world--home, school, work, play. Having faced death we can laugh--the laughter of hope and faith in the Lord of life. The laughter of the living. And I remember well that Myrtle really knew how to laugh. I am the resurrection and the life. Whoever believes in me will never die. Amen.

Harper Bruce Thompson was buried in 1981 in Woodlawn Memorial Gardens, Harrisburg, Dauphin County, Pennsylvania, USA[8]. His cause of death was Cardiorespiratory arrest w/subdural hematoma[7]. He was counted in the census in 1910 in Porter, Schuylkill County, Pennsylvania, USA[17]. He was counted in the census in 1920 in Porter, Schuylkill County, Pennsylvania, USA[18, 19]. He was counted in the census in 1930 in Emmaus, Lehigh County, Pennsylvania(Uncle James Knittle)[20]. He was counted in the census in 1940 in Tower City, Schuylkill County, Pennsylvania, USA[12]. He was educated at School in 1920[21]. He had a medical condition of cardiac arrest due to clot in brain, cataracts, heart disease, hernia. He was employed as a Boxer about Abt. 1929. He was employed as a Lineman (Telephone Co) in 1930[20]. He was employed as a Laborer in 1935. He was employed as a Bell Telephone Co in 1940 in Lineman. He was employed as a Retired mail handler (Harrisburg Post Office) in 1981[8]. He was affiliated with the Lutheran religion. He lived in 914 ? St., Emmaus, Lehigh County, Pennsylvania, USA in 1930[20]. He lived in 335 Main St, Tower City, Pennsylvania, USA in 1940[12]. He lived in Harrisburg, Dauphin County, Pennsylvania, USA in 1972[22]. He lived in Beaufort Farms, Camp Curtain, Estherton, Fort Hunter, Harrisburg, Hecktown, Lucknow, Rockville, Uptown, Windsor farms, all Dauphin County, Pennsylvania, USA in 1981[23]. He lived in 2600 Green St., Harrisburg, Dauphin County, Pennsylvania, USA in 1981[7]. His Social Security Number was 205-05-3254[23]. Funeral: 1981 in Jesse H Geigle, 2100 Linglestown Rd.,Harrisburg, Dauphin County, Pennsylvania, USA[8] Funeral: 1981 (Lakeside Lutheran Church[8]) Political Party: in Republican

Notes for Harper Bruce Thompson:
Harper was named for his grandfather, Robert "Bruce" Thompson.

Funeral of Harper Thompson
Pastor Gregory Harbaugh, John 11:17-44, July 1981
Harper Thompson, 73, died Thursday at Polyclinic Hospital. He was a member of Lakeside Lutheran Church. A former Postal Service employee, Mr. Thompson is survived by his wife Myrtle, and 3 sons Eugene, Gerald and Robert, and 10 grandchildren and 2 great grandchildren. Services will be held…and so on reads the obituary. And that's all it says. But what about the man, the husband, the father, the brother, grandfather and friend? That's the person you and I have known. A tall, rugged-looking man who sometimes cried at

movies, who was sensitive to others, and friendly. I only knew Harper for two years, but I won't forget him. Every Sunday when he and Myrtle were in church, I could depend on hearing Harper's deep baritone, 'Hi ya Gregg!' as the tall man walked by and shook my hand. I remember, too, the man in the hospital who got. teary-eyed talking about his sons - 'good sons' he would say; who nearly beamed when Myrtle was near. And who cried when he received communion. You have memories, too. Some fonder than others, I suspect. Some of joy and fun. Others, perhaps, of father angry with erring boys. Of a husband maybe working too hard or worried about bills. Others of Harper's broad smile and great laugh. Of dad playing with his 'boys. You remember, too. That's Harper. For him we grieve. For him we weep. Because we loved him and will miss him. Like Jesus and Lazarus. A good friend. Dead. So he mourned. But the question came "Could not the one who opened the eyes of the blind kept this man from dying?" That's our question too, I think, if we really face up to our grief. "Why couldn't God keep Harper alive and well?" Though death comes to each of us, the timing could usually do better. So we not only weep but we are somewhat angry as well: with hospitals, doctors and a God who didn't seem to help. Yet in the midst of our grief and anger comes a word, a story, of life and hope that overcome death and sorrow. "I am the resurrection and the life - unbind him and let him go." Lazarus was raised - a sign to John's church that resurrection is not only for the end-time but happens now - in the midst of life and death, joy and sorrow - new life, restored life comes into our world. As we may loosen and let go of the bonds of death and the past. Harper, unlike Lazarus, will not rise and walk among us. Lazarus was for John's church and for us a sign that life overcomes death. We have the sign. Yet not only that. For Jesus' own death and resurrection stand before us - cross and empty tomb - not only as sign but as gift and power. For we, like Harper, who are baptized have taken part in that death and resurrection - washed in it, enlivened through it, "I am the resurrection and the life" said Jesus. Yet he wept and grieved as we do. But death and grief are not final. God has the last word and the last laugh. We are resurrection and life in the midst of Sorrow and death. For God is with us, inseparable from us and Harper. We remember him. And we untie him, to let him go. For us there is life now. There is more to give and to receive. There is time for joy and laughter. We remember Harper. But we also hope - as the communion of saints and in the resurrection of the dead

- for nothing, not even death, can separate him or us from God's love in Christ Jesus. I am the resurrection and the life.

Generation 2

2. **James "Edward" Batdorf** (son of Thomas Edward Batdorf and Mary Louisa Peters) was born on February 15, 1885 in Loyalton, Dauphin County, Pennsylvania, USA[24, 25, 26, 27]. He died on August 19, 1954 in Home, Lykens, Dauphin County, Pennsylvania, USA[24]. He married **Beulah Irene Wert** (daughter of John Henry Wert and Adeline Row) on February 8, 1908 in Oakdale Evangelical, Dauphin County, Pennsylvania, USA[5, 28].

3. **Beulah Irene Wert** (daughter of John Henry Wert and Adeline Row) was born on December 31, 1889 in Elizabethville, Dauphin County, Pennsylvania, USA[29]. She died on June 10, 1983 in Dr. Convalescence Center, Selinsgrove, Snyder County, Pennsylvania, USA[29, 30, 31].

James "Edward" Batdorf was baptized on June 6, 1886 in Oakdale Evangelical Circuit, Dauphin County, Pennsylvania, USA[5, 32]. He was buried in 1954 (Loyalton EUB Church, Loyalton, Dauphin, PA[33]). He was buried on August 23, 1954 in Calvary (Union) United Methodist, Wiconisco, Dauphin County, Pennsylvania, USA[24, 33]. His cause of death was Coronary occlusion w/hypertension w/diabetes mellitus[24]. He was counted in the census in 1900 in Washington, Dauphin County, Pennsylvania, USA[34]. He was counted in the census in 1910 in Washington, Dauphin County, Pennsylvania, USA[35]. He was counted in the census in 1920 in Washington, ,Pennsylvania, USA[10]. He was counted in the census in 1930 in Lykens, Dauphin County, Pennsylvania, USA[36]. He was counted in the census in 1940 in Lykens, Dauphin County, Pennsylvania, USA[37]. His height was 5 ft. 6 in.. He had a medical condition of Short height, Medium build, Brown eyes, ? gray hair [1917]
Gray eyes, Brown hair, Light complexion, Height 5'6", Weight 143# [1942]. He was employed as a Day laborer in 1900[34]. He was employed as a Miner in 1908[28]. He was employed as a Miner (Coalminer) in 1910[40]. He was employed as a Miner (Susquehanna

Colliery Co) in 1918[38]. He was employed as a Miner (Coal mine) in 1920[41]. He was employed as a Miner (Lykens Coal Co) about Abt. 1925[42]. He was employed as a Laborer (Coal washery) in 1930[11]. He was employed as a Laborer in 1935[2]. He was employed as a Road & ? Construction Yard in 1940 in Laborer[37]. He was employed as a WPA (Harrisburg, Dauphin County, Pennsylvania, USA) in 1942[38]. He was employed as a Labor (Lykens Borough) in 1954[24]. His estate was probated in 1954. He was affiliated with the Methodist religion. He was affiliated with the Methodist < Evangelical United Brethren < Evangelical religion. He lived in Loyalton, Dauphin County, Pennsylvania, USA in 1918[38]. He lived in Loyalton, Dauphin County, Pennsylvania, USA in 1918[38]. He lived in State Road 199, Washington Tp., Dauphin County, Pennsylvania, USA in 1920[41]. He lived in 480 North St., Lykens, Dauphin County, Pennsylvania, USA in 1930[13]. He lived in 542 North Street, Lykens, Dauphin County, Pennsylvania, USA in 1942[38]. He lived in 542 North St., Lykens, Dauphin County, Pennsylvania, USA in 1954[24, 33]. His Social Security Number was 205-09-5145[24]. His weight was 143 lb. 0 oz.. Funeral: 1954 in John R. Shultz Funeral Home, 406 Market St., Lykens, Dauphin County, Pennsylvania, USA[43] Funeral: 1954 in Reiff? Helt?, 523 W. Main St., Lykens, Dauphin County, Pennsylvania, USA[33, 44]

Notes for James "Edward" Batdorf:
James was name for and nicknamed Edward after his father, Thomas "Edward" Batdorf.

Beulah Irene Wert was baptized on May 18, 1890 in St. Johns (Hill) Lutheran, Berrysburg, Dauphin County, Pennsylvania, USA[5]. She was buried in 1983 (St. Christopher Evangelical Lutheran Church[31]). She was buried on June 14, 1983 in Calvary (Union) United Methodist, Wiconisco, Dauphin County, Pennsylvania, USA[29]. Her cause of death was Acute congestive cardiac failure w/poss. brain stem CVA & ASCVD[29]. She was counted in the census in 1900 in Washington, Dauphin County, Pennsylvania, USA[45]. She was counted in the census in 1910 in Washington, Dauphin County, Pennsylvania, USA. She was counted in the census in 1920 in Washington, Dauphin County, Pennsylvania, USA. She was counted in the census in 1930 in Lykens, Dauphin County, Pennsylvania,

USA. She was counted in the census in 1940 in Lykens, Dauphin County, Pennsylvania, USA[37]. She was educated at School in 1900[45]. She was employed as a Dressmaker (at home) in 1920[41]. She was employed as a Housewife in 1935[2]. She was employed as a Wallpaperer about Abt. 1950. She was employed as a Seamstress (Clothing) in 1983[29]. She was affiliated with the Lutheran religion. She was affiliated with the Methodist religion. She lived in Harrisburg, Dauphin County, Pennsylvania, USA in 1956[46]. She lived in Dauphin County, Pennsylvania, USA in 1983. She lived in 800 Broad St., Selinsgrove, Snyder County, Pennsylvania, USA17870 in 1983[29]. She lived in Big Run, Coaldale, Erdman, Germantown, Loyalton, Lykens, Specktown, all Dauphin County, Pennsylvania, USA in 1983[30]. Her Social Security Number was 162-22-1417[29, 30]. Funeral: 1983 in Schultz Funeral Home, 406 Market St., Lykens, Dauphin County, Pennsylvania, USA[29, 31]

Beulah Irene Wert and James "Edward" Batdorf had the following children:

i. Alvin Leroy Batdorf (son of James "Edward" Batdorf and Beulah Irene Wert) was born in 1908 in Pennsylvania, USA. He died in 1972[47]. He married Margaret Elizabeth Marlow. She was born in 1908 in Pennsylvania, USA. She died in 2004 in Pennsylvania, USA[48].

ii. Margaret Irene Batdorf (daughter of James "Edward" Batdorf and Beulah Irene Wert) was born on December 5, 1909 in Pennsylvania, USA. She died in December 1990 in Wiconisco, Dauphin County, Pennsylvania, USA. She married Albert Forrest Kohler. He was born in 1908. He died in 1991[47].

iii. Mildred Catherine Batdorf (daughter of James "Edward" Batdorf and Beulah Irene Wert) was born in 1912 in Pennsylvania, USA. She died in June 2010 in Herndon, Dauphin County, Pennsylvania, USA. She married Thomas Randall Moon. He died in 1960.

Notes for Mildred Catherine Batdorf:
Mildred Batdorf Moon

by Marc D. Thompson
as told by Mildred Moon, January 1999
Mildred was born Mildred Catherine Batdorf on January 29, 1911 the daughter of Beulah Wert and James "Edward" Batdorf. She was the sister of my grandmother Myrtle, Alvin, Margaret, Harry, Ruth and Romaine. Mildred and Myrtle were born and raised in Big Run, Pennsylvania. Their mother Beulah was the daughter of John and Adaline Wert of Big Run. The Wert family farmed and "were hard-working people." James Edward was the son of Thomas and Mary Batdorf, also of Big Run. Their "grandmother Batdorf was a housewife and grandfather Batdorf was a farmer and worked in the mines." Myrtle and Mildred "lived in a two-story house and ate in the kitchen." Their home was heated by coal and they did not have a fireplace. The family did not always have electricity, as candles, kerosene and coal were used. The home had a cellar and water was retrieved from a well. Mail was delivered by rural route and they "had a cat named Blacky." Mildred was the fourth child born and Myrtle was the youngest of the seven children. As a child, their major chore, among others, was doing the dishes. Their mother did the cooking and ironing and she taught them to sew, crochet, knit and embroider. Mildred learned to drive a car from a neighborhood boy and her husband Randall Moon taught her to cook. Mildred and Myrtle's father, Edward Batdorf, was a miner and Mildred worked to help contribute to the family income. She was fourteen years old when she secured her first job. The family had a garden and they "dug the ground and got it ready to plant. They grew potatoes, lettuce, celery, onions, tomatoes, peppers, cabbage and a lot more." They had cherry and peach trees. Their mother did canning and raised chickens and the family often ate beef, pork and chicken. Her parents and siblings did all the work, hiring no one to help with the house, garden or animals. "Saturday was the day that you got a rest for the weekend and Sunday we got ready for church." The family attended a little church in Loyalton. For Christmas they would wake up early to see the tree and they received clothes as gifts. On July Fourth, "my brother

had a birthday and we had games that we played." In general, however, sibling's birthdays were just another day. For her birthday, Mildred received clothes made by her mother. The family did not entertain often but they did go to family picnics. She kept in touch with distant family and visited relatives often. In the summer, "we sat under a nice shade tree to keep cool" and in the winter kept warm with long johns. Mildred recalls one extreme winter storm when the snow reached up over the fences. For recreation, the children played jump rope, ball and cards. Mildred's best friend was Hilda Buffington and they often played games for fun. Mildred did not learn to swim and the family never went on vacation. Growing up, there was no place to shop so the family ordered items from "men who came around and the next day he came with it." They never went to the city to shop but there was a small country store. Lykens was the largest town nearby and Mildred used to take the train to visit her grandmother in Elizabethville. My father "got a car when I was ten years old. It was a Ford model T." Mildred attended a little red one-room schoolhouse in Big Run. It was only two houses away and she usually walked to school alone. Mildred was closest to her mother and she admired her father most. When young, Mildred "hoped to be a good housekeeper." Her family supported and encouraged her and they influenced her and helped her develop skills. When asked if she would choose the same career path, she said, "No. I would choose for a better life." "I met my husband in Lykens. I was engaged on Easter and married on October 1, 1926." Mildred was married in Hagerstown to her husband, a dentist, and her children were born in…(remainder missing)

iv. Harry Franklin Batdorf (son of James "Edward" Batdorf and Beulah Irene Wert) was born on July 21, 1912 in Pennsylvania, USA. He died in August 1977 in Lykens, Dauphin County, Pennsylvania, USA[47]. He married Grace Naomi Hoy. She was born in 1915. She died in 1962[47].

1. v. Myrtle Adeline Batdorf (daughter of James "Edward"

Batdorf and Beulah Irene Wert) was born on January 5, 1918 in Big Run, Dauphin County, Pennsylvania, USA[1, 2]. She died on May 8, 1983 in Polyclinic Hospital, Harrisburg, Dauphin County, Pennsylvania, USA[3, 4]. She married Harper Bruce Thompson (son of Abel Robert Thompson and Augusta "Gussie" Mae Hensel) on June 15, 1935 in St. Johns (Hill) Lutheran, Berrysburg, Dauphin County, Pennsylvania, USA[2, 5]. He was born on September 28, 1907 in Sheridan, Schuylkill County, Pennsylvania, USA[6, 7, 8]. He died on July 23, 1981 in Polyclinic Hospital, Harrisburg, Dauphin County, Pennsylvania, USA[7, 8].

vi. Ruth E Batdorf (daughter of James "Edward" Batdorf and Beulah Irene Wert) was born on April 29, 1923 in Pennsylvania, USA. She died on August 16, 2006 in Ridgeway, Elk County, Pennsylvania, USA. She married Claude M Reed. He was born in 1921. He died in 1986[47].

vii. Romaine Batdorf (daughter of James "Edward" Batdorf and Beulah Irene Wert) was born on May 24, 1925 in Pennsylvania, USA. She died in July 1981 in Lykens, Dauphin County, Pennsylvania, USA. She married Clarence "Bess" D Messner. He was born in 1925. He died in 2005.

Generation 3

4. **Thomas Edward Batdorf** (son of Peter Batdorf and Elizabeth Welker) was born on July 2, 1851 in Big Run, Dauphin County, Pennsylvania, USA[49, 50]. He died on August 13, 1913 in Elizabethville, Dauphin County, Pennsylvania, USA[50]. He married **Mary Louisa Peters** (daughter of Samuel Peters and Mary Ann Swartz) on December 6, 1874 in Rev. W.G. Engle, Dauphin County, Pennsylvania, USA[5].

5. **Mary Louisa Peters** (daughter of Samuel Peters and Mary Ann Swartz) was born on March 31, 1858 in Mifflin, Dauphin County, Pennsylvania, USA[49, 51]. She died on August 3, 1924 in Home, Elizabethville, Dauphin County, Pennsylvania, USA[5, 49].

Thomas Edward Batdorf was baptized on October 12, 1851 in St.

Peters (Hoffmans) Reformed, Loyalton, Dauphin County, Pennsylvania, USA[5]. He was buried on August 16, 1916 in St. Johns (Oakdale) Cemetery, Loyalton, Dauphin County, Pennsylvania, USA[50]. His cause of death was Mitral insufficiency & Bright's disease (ie, Chronic inflammation) of kidneys w/[50]. He was counted in the census in 1860 in Lykens, Dauphin County, Pennsylvania, USA[52]. He was counted in the census in 1870 in Berrysburg, Dauphin County, Pennsylvania, USA(Wise)[53]. He was counted in the census in 1880 in Washington, Dauphin County, Pennsylvania, USA[54]. He was counted in the census in 1900 in Washington, Dauphin County, Pennsylvania, USA[34]. He was counted in the census in 1910 in Elizabethville, Dauphin County, Pennsylvania, USA[55]. He was educated at School in 1860[52]. His height was 6 ft. 0 in.. He served in the military between 1861-1865 (Civil War). He was employed as a Apprentice to Blacksmith in 1870[53]. He was employed as a Laborer in 1880[54]. He was employed as a Coal miner in 1900[34]. He was employed as a Retired laborer in 1910[55]. He was employed as a Laborer in 1916[50]. He was affiliated with the Methodist religion. He was affiliated with the Methodist < Evangelical United Brethren < Evangelical religion. He was affiliated with the Reformed religion. He lived in W. Main St., Elizabethville, Dauphin County, Pennsylvania, USA in 1910[56]. Funeral: 1916 in Buffington Funeral Home, Elizabethville, Dauphin County, Pennsylvania, USA[50]

Notes for Thomas Edward Batdorf:
Thomas was named after his uncle "Thomas" Batdorf.

Mary Louisa Peters was buried on August 6, 1924 in St. Johns (Oakdale) Cemetery, Loyalton, Dauphin County, Pennsylvania, USA[51]. Her cause of death was Cerebral hemorrhage[51]. She was counted in the census in 1860 in Mifflin, Dauphin County, Pennsylvania, USA[57]. She was counted in the census in 1870. She was counted in the census in 1880 in Washington, Dauphin County, Pennsylvania, USA. She was counted in the census in 1900 in Washington, Dauphin County, Pennsylvania, USA. She was counted in the census in 1910 in Elizabethville, Dauphin County, Pennsylvania, USA. She was counted in the census in 1920 in Elizabethville, Dauphin County, Pennsylvania, USA[58]. Her height was

4 ft. 12 in.. She was employed as a Keeping house in 1880[54]. She was employed as a Housekeeper in 1924[51]. She was affiliated with the Methodist religion. She was affiliated with the Methodist < Evangelical United Brethren < Evangelical[42] religion. She lived in Main St., Elizabethville, Dauphin County, Pennsylvania, USA in 1920[59]. Funeral: 1924 in Buffington Funeral Home, Elizabethville, Dauphin County, Pennsylvania, USA[51]

Notes for Mary Louisa Peters:
Mary was named for her mother "Mary" Ann Swartz.

Mary Louisa Peters and Thomas Edward Batdorf had the following children:

    i.   George Batdorf (son of Thomas Edward Batdorf and Mary Louisa Peters) was born in 1875 in Pennsylvania, USA. He died in 1881.

    ii.   Kirby Batdorf (son of Thomas Edward Batdorf and Mary Louisa Peters) was born in 1877 in Pennsylvania, USA. He died in 1881.

    iii.   John Batdorf (son of Thomas Edward Batdorf and Mary Louisa Peters) was born on September 7, 1878 in Pennsylvania, USA. He died in January 1968 in Annville, Lebanon County, Pennsylvania, USA.

    iv.   William Batdorf (son of Thomas Edward Batdorf and Mary Louisa Peters) was born in 1880 in Pennsylvania, USA. He married Anna "Annie" ?. She was born in 1874 in Pennsylvania, USA.

    v.   Mary Ellen Batdorf (daughter of Thomas Edward Batdorf and Mary Louisa Peters) was born in 1881 in Pennsylvania, USA. She died in 1963.

    vi.   Adam Scorvella Batdorf (son of Thomas Edward Batdorf and Mary Louisa Peters) was born in 1882 in Pennsylvania, USA. He died in 1952. He married Caroline "Carrie" May Boyer. She was born in 1884 in Pennsylvania, USA. She died in 1973[47].

2. vii. James "Edward" Batdorf (son of Thomas Edward Batdorf and Mary Louisa Peters) was born on February 15, 1885 in Loyalton, Dauphin County, Pennsylvania, USA[24, 25, 26, 27]. He died on August 19, 1954 in Home, Lykens, Dauphin County, Pennsylvania, USA[24]. He married Beulah Irene Wert (daughter of John Henry Wert and Adeline Row) on February 8, 1908 in Oakdale Evangelical, Dauphin County, Pennsylvania, USA[5, 28]. She was born on December 31, 1889 in Elizabethville, Dauphin County, Pennsylvania, USA[29]. She died on June 10, 1983 in Dr. Convalescence Center, Selinsgrove, Snyder County, Pennsylvania, USA[29, 30, 31].

   viii. Oscar Newton Batdorf (son of Thomas Edward Batdorf and Mary Louisa Peters) was born on August 15, 1886 in Loyalton, Dauphin County, Pennsylvania, USA. He died in August 1981 in Sarasota, Sarasota County, FL. He married Mabel Susan Elizabeth Motter. She was born in 1887 in Pennsylvania, USA.

   ix. Frances I Batdorf (daughter of Thomas Edward Batdorf and Mary Louisa Peters) was born in 1887 in Pennsylvania, USA. She married Samuel W Lentz. He was born in 1886. He died in 1940[47].

   x. Joseph Warren Batdorf (son of Thomas Edward Batdorf and Mary Louisa Peters) was born in 1888 in Elizabethtown, Dauphin County, Pennsylvania, USA. He died in 1928[47].

   xi. Harvey Clarence Batdorf (son of Thomas Edward Batdorf and Mary Louisa Peters) was born in 1891 in Loyalton, Dauphin County, Pennsylvania, USA. He died in 1949[47]. He married Susan Elizabeth Bahney. She was born in 1896 in Pennsylvania, USA.

   xii. Cora Annette Batdorf (daughter of Thomas Edward Batdorf and Mary Louisa Peters) was born on April 18, 1892 in Pennsylvania, USA. She died in May 1981 in Harrisburg, Dauphin County, Pennsylvania, USA[47]. She married

Herbert Eugene Buffington. He was born in 1888. He died in 1959[47].

xiii. Stella Louisa Batdorf (daughter of Thomas Edward Batdorf and Mary Louisa Peters) was born in 1893 in Pennsylvania, USA. She died in 1981. She married Lafayette DeWees. He was born in 1883. He died in 1981[47]. She married ? Paul.

xiv Charlotte "Lottie" F Batdorf (daughter of Thomas Edward Batdorf and Mary Louisa Peters) was born in 1895 in Pennsylvania, USA.

xv. Norman Batdorf (son of Thomas Edward Batdorf and Mary Louisa Peters) was born in 1896 in Pennsylvania, USA. He died in 1896.

xvi. Alvin Thomas Batdorf (son of Thomas Edward Batdorf and Mary Louisa Peters) was born in 1898 in Pennsylvania, USA. He died in 1898.

xvii. Verna A Batdorf (daughter of Thomas Edward Batdorf and Mary Louisa Peters) was born on June 2, 1899 in Pennsylvania, USA. She died in December 1992 in Sherman Oaks, Los Angeles County, CA. She married Leon Washington Shultz. He was born in 1890.

6. **John Henry Wert** (son of David M Wert and Catherine Shoop) was born on December 23, 1855 in Northumberland County, Pennsylvania, USA[60]. He died on October 30, 1924 in Harrisburg Hospital, Harrisburg, Dauphin County, Pennsylvania, USA[60]. He married **Adeline Row** (daughter of Daniel Row and Susan Frantz) about Abt. 1878 in Dauphin County, Pennsylvania, USA.

7. **Adeline Row** (daughter of Daniel Row and Susan Frantz) was born on January 2, 1860 in Dauphin County, Pennsylvania, USA[61, 62, 63]. She died on March 6, 1921 in Harrisburg, Dauphin County, Pennsylvania, USA[62].

John Henry Wert was baptized on December 23, 1855 in Northumberland Co?, Pennsylvania, USA. He was buried on November 2, 1924 in St. Johns (Hill) Lutheran, Berrysburg, Dauphin County, Pennsylvania, USA[60, 64]. His cause of death was Hemorrhage & shock from fractured ribs & other abd. injuries...rolling timber.[60]. He was counted in the census in 1860 in Lower Mahanoy, Northumberland County, Pennsylvania, USA[65]. He was counted in the census in 1870 in Lykens, Dauphin County, Pennsylvania, USA[66]. He was counted in the census in 1880 in Washington, Dauphin County, Pennsylvania, USA[67]. He was counted in the census in 1900 in Washington, Dauphin County, Pennsylvania, USA[45]. He was counted in the census in 1910 in Washington, Dauphin County, Pennsylvania, USA(enumerated twice)[68]. He was counted in the census in 1920 in Washington, Dauphin County, Pennsylvania, USA[69]. His height was 6 ft. 0 in.. He was employed as a Blacksmith in 1880[67]. He was employed as a Day laborer in 1900[45]. He was employed as a Laborer (?) in 1910[68]. He was employed as a Laborer (Coal mine) in 1920[70]. He was employed as a Timber laborer (Susquehanna Colliery) in 1924[60]. His estate was probated between November 19, 1924-1938 in Washington Township, Dauphin County, Pennsylvania, USA(listed in index only)[71]. He was affiliated with the Lutheran religion. He lived in State Road 199, Washington, Dauphin County, Pennsylvania, USA in 1920[70]. Funeral: 1924 in Buffington Funeral Home, Elizabethville, Dauphin County, Pennsylvania, USA[60]

Notes for John Henry Wert:
John was named for his grandfather "John" Shoop and his uncle "Henry" Wert.

Adeline Row was baptized on March 11, 1860 in St. Johns (Hill) Lutheran, Berrysburg, Dauphin County, Pennsylvania, USA[61]. She was buried on March 10, 1921 in St. Johns (Hill) Lutheran, Berrysburg, Dauphin County, Pennsylvania, USA[62]. Her cause of death was Sero-fibrinous pleurisy w/myocarditis[62]. She was counted in the census in 1860 in Washington, Dauphin County, Pennsylvania, USA[72]. She was counted in the census in 1870 in Wiconisco, Dauphin County, Pennsylvania, USA[73]. She was counted in the census in 1880 in Washington, Dauphin County, Pennsylvania, USA.

She was counted in the census in 1900 in Washington, Dauphin County, Pennsylvania, USA. She was counted in the census in 1910 in Washington, Dauphin County, Pennsylvania, USA. She was counted in the census in 1920 in Washington, Dauphin County, Pennsylvania, USA. She was educated at School in 1870[73]. Her height was 5 ft. 5 in.. She was employed as a Keeping house in 1880[67]. She was employed as a Owned farm about Abt. 1900[42]. She was employed as a Housewife in 1921[62]. She was affiliated with the Lutheran[42] religion. She lived in Lykens, Dauphin County, Pennsylvania, USA in 1921[62]. Funeral: 1921 in Buffington Funeral Home, Elizabethville, Dauphin County, Pennsylvania, USA[62]

Adeline Row and John Henry Wert had the following children:

    i.   Caroline "Carrie" Catherine Wert (daughter of John Henry Wert and Adeline Row) was born in 1880 in Pennsylvania, USA.

    ii.   Harriet "Hattie" May Wert (daughter of John Henry Wert and Adeline Row) was born in 1881 in Pennsylvania, USA. She married Daniel George Romberger. He was born in 1879 in Pennsylvania, USA. He died in 1959[74].

    iii.   ? Wert (child of John Henry Wert and Adeline Row) was born about Abt. 1883 in Pennsylvania, USA.

    iv.   Florence Stella Wert (daughter of John Henry Wert and Adeline Row) was born on March 6, 1886 in Pennsylvania, USA. She died in November 1972 in Elizabethville, Dauphin County, Pennsylvania, USA. She married John Adam Kocher. He was born in 1872 in Pennsylvania, USA.

3.   v.   Beulah Irene Wert (daughter of John Henry Wert and Adeline Row) was born on December 31, 1889 in Elizabethville, Dauphin County, Pennsylvania, USA[29]. She died on June 10, 1983 in Dr. Convalescence Center, Selinsgrove, Snyder County, Pennsylvania, USA[29, 30, 31]. She married James "Edward" Batdorf (son of Thomas Edward Batdorf and Mary Louisa Peters) on February 8, 1908 in Oakdale Evangelical, Dauphin County, Pennsylvania, USA[5, 28]. He was born on February 15, 1885

in Loyalton, Dauphin County, Pennsylvania, USA[24, 25, 26, 27].
He died on August 19, 1954 in Home, Lykens, Dauphin
County, Pennsylvania, USA[24].

vi. Margaret Wert (daughter of John Henry Wert and Adeline
Row) was born in 1904 in Pennsylvania, USA. She married
John M Naughton. He was born in 1899.

Generation 4

8. **Peter Batdorf** (son of Jacob Peter Batdorf and Maria Catherine
Steiner) was born on January 20, 1814 in Lykens, Dauphin County,
Pennsylvania, USA[49, 75, 76, 77, 78]. He died on December 5, 1880 in
Lykens, Dauphin County, Pennsylvania, USA[49, 75, 76, 77, 78, 79, 80]. He
married **Elizabeth Welker** (daughter of John Welker and Maria
Elizabeth Messerschmidt) about Abt. 1831 in Dauphin County,
Pennsylvania, USA.

9. **Elizabeth Welker** (daughter of John Welker and Maria Elizabeth
Messerschmidt) was born on November 23, 1812 in Lykens, Dauphin
County, Pennsylvania, USA[49, 75, 76]. She died on July 7, 1868 in
Lykens, Dauphin County, Pennsylvania, USA[49, 75, 76, 81].

Peter Batdorf was baptized on February 27, 1814 in St. Peters
(Hoffman) Reformed, Loyalton, Dauphin County, Pennsylvania,
USA[49]. He was buried in 1880 in St. Peters (Hoffman) Reformed,
Loyalton, Dauphin County, Pennsylvania, USA[49, 75, 76, 77]. He was
counted in the census in 1820 in Lykens, Dauphin County,
Pennsylvania, USA (w/father[82]). He was counted in the census in
1830 in Lykens, Dauphin County, Pennsylvania, USA (w/mother[83]).
He was counted in the census in 1840 in Lykens, Dauphin County,
Pennsylvania, USA[84, 85]. He was counted in the census in 1850 in
Lykens, Dauphin County, Pennsylvania, USA[86]. He was counted in
the census in 1860 in Lykens, Dauphin County, Pennsylvania, USA[52].
He was counted in the census in 1870 in Lykens, Dauphin County,
Pennsylvania, USA[87]. He was counted in the census in 1880 in
Lykens, Dauphin County, Pennsylvania, USA[88]. He was employed as
a Yeoman about Abt. 1840. He was employed as a Carpenter
between 1850-1870[86]. He was employed as a Farmer in 1880[88]. His
estate was probated on January 4, 1881 in Dauphin County,
Pennsylvania, USA[80]. He was affiliated with the Reformed religion.

Notes for Peter Batdorf:
Peter was named after his father Jacob "Peter" Batdorf.

Elizabeth Welker was buried in 1868 in St. Peters (Hoffman) Reformed, Loyalton, Dauphin County, Pennsylvania, USA[76]. She was counted in the census in 1820 in Lykens, Dauphin County, Pennsylvania, USA (w/father[89]). She was counted in the census in 1830 in Lykens, Dauphin County, Pennsylvania, USA (w/father[90]). She was counted in the census in 1840 in Lykens, Dauphin County, Pennsylvania, USA (w/husband). She was counted in the census in 1850 in Lykens, Dauphin County, Pennsylvania, USA. She was counted in the census in 1860 in Lykens, Dauphin County, Pennsylvania, USA. She was employed as a Homemaker about Abt. 1840. Her estate was probated about Abt. 1854 in Elizabeth was not mentioned in father's will[91]. She was affiliated with the Reformed religion.

Notes for Elizabeth Welker:
Elizabeth was named after her mother Maria "Elizabeth" Messerschmidt.

Elizabeth Welker and Peter Batdorf had the following children:

    i.   Esther Batdorf (daughter of Peter Batdorf and Elizabeth Welker) was born in 1836 in Pennsylvania, USA.

    ii.   Jonas Batdorf (son of Peter Batdorf and Elizabeth Welker) was born in 1837 in Pennsylvania, USA. He married Lucetta Rickert. She was born in 1840. She died in 1867[48].

    iii.   Elizabeth Batdorf (daughter of Peter Batdorf and Elizabeth Welker) was born in 1839 in Pennsylvania, USA. She married Joseph Russell. He was born in 1836. He died in 1901[48].

    iv.   Susan Batdorf (daughter of Peter Batdorf and Elizabeth Welker) was born in 1842 in Pennsylvania, USA. She married ? Miller.

v. John William Batdorf (son of Peter Batdorf and Elizabeth Welker) was born in 1844 in Pennsylvania, USA. He died in 1921. He married Sarah Miller. She was born in 1842 in Pennsylvania, USA.

vi. Sarah Batdorf (daughter of Peter Batdorf and Elizabeth Welker) was born in 1845 in Pennsylvania, USA. She died in 1922. She married James H Smith. He was born in 1845. He died in 1904[48].

vii. Peter S Batdorf (son of Peter Batdorf and Elizabeth Welker) was born in 1848 in Pennsylvania, USA. He married Mary Elizabeth Sierer. She was born in 1853 in Pennsylvania, USA.

viii. Anna Batdorf (daughter of Peter Batdorf and Elizabeth Welker) was born about Abt. 1850 in Pennsylvania, USA.

ix. Rebecca Batdorf (daughter of Peter Batdorf and Elizabeth Welker) was born about Abt. 1850 in Pennsylvania, USA.

4. x. Thomas Edward Batdorf (son of Peter Batdorf and Elizabeth Welker) was born on July 2, 1851 in Big Run, Dauphin County, Pennsylvania, USA[49, 50]. He died on August 13, 1913 in Elizabethville, Dauphin County, Pennsylvania, USA[50]. He married Mary Louisa Peters (daughter of Samuel Peters and Mary Ann Swartz) on December 6, 1874 in Rev. W.G. Engle, Dauphin County, Pennsylvania, USA[5]. She was born on March 31, 1858 in Mifflin, Dauphin County, Pennsylvania, USA[49, 51]. She died on August 3, 1924 in Home, Elizabethville, Dauphin County, Pennsylvania, USA[5, 49].

xi. Louisa Batdorf (daughter of Peter Batdorf and Elizabeth Welker) was born in 1854 in Pennsylvania, USA. She married William Frantz. He was born about Abt. 1850.

10. **Samuel Peters** (son of John Peters and Anna Maria ?) was born in 1821 in Buffalo, Union County, Pennsylvania, USA. He died between

1860-1870 in Perry County, Pennsylvania, USA. He married **Mary Ann Swartz** (daughter of John Swartz and Anna ?) about Abt. 1840 in Union County, Pennsylvania, USA.

11. **Mary Ann Swartz** (daughter of John Swartz and Anna ?) was born on January 5, 1820 in Juniata, Perry County, Pennsylvania, USA[92]. She died on August 9, 1897 in Washington, Dauphin County, Pennsylvania, USA[93, 94].

Samuel Peters was buried between 1860-1870 in Perry County, Pennsylvania, USA. He was counted in the census in 1830 in Buffalo, Union County, Pennsylvania, USA (w/father[95]). He was counted in the census in 1840 in Buffalo, Union County, Pennsylvania, USA (w/grandfather Peters[96]). He was counted in the census in 1850 in Union, Union County, Pennsylvania, USA[97, 98]. He was counted in the census in 1860 in Mifflin, Dauphin County, Pennsylvania, USA[57]. He was employed as a Laborer in 1850[97, 98]. He was employed as a Laborer in 1860[57].

Mary Ann Swartz was buried on August 12, 1897 in St. Johns (Oakdale) Cemetery, Loyalton, Dauphin County, Pennsylvania, USA[93, 99]. Her cause of death was Heart disease[94]. She was counted in the census in 1820 in Juniata, Perry, Pennsylvania (w/father[100]). She was counted in the census in 1830 in Juniata, Perry County, Pennsylvania, USA (w/father[101, 102]). She was counted in the census in 1840[103]. She was counted in the census in 1850 in Union, Union County, Pennsylvania, USA. She was counted in the census in 1860 in Mifflin, Dauphin County, Pennsylvania, USA. She was counted in the census in 1870 in Lykens, Dauphin County, Pennsylvania, USA[104]. She was counted in the census in 1880 in Washington, Dauphin County, Pennsylvania, USA(Row)[105]. She was employed as a Keeping house in 1870[104]. She was employed as a Retired house keeper in 1880[105].

Notes for Mary Ann Swartz:
Birth could be Juniata Tp or Juniata Co, Pennsylvania [Mary Peters death cert, Bk C, #945, 1897, Dauphin County Register of Wills,

Harrisburg, PA]

Mary Ann Swartz and Samuel Peters had the following children:

i. John A Peters (son of Samuel Peters and Mary Ann Swartz) was born in 1844 in Pennsylvania, USA. He died in 1922. He married Mary ?. She was born in 1848 in Pennsylvania, USA.

ii. Emma C Peters (daughter of Samuel Peters and Mary Ann Swartz) was born in 1846 in Pennsylvania, USA.

iii. Jonathan M Peters (son of Samuel Peters and Mary Ann Swartz) was born in July 1849 in Pennsylvania, USA. He died in 1918. He married Elizabeth ?. She was born in March 1854 in Pennsylvania, USA.

iv. Matthew Peters (son of Samuel Peters and Mary Ann Swartz) was born in 1849 in Pennsylvania, USA.

v. Matilda "Tillie" Peters (daughter of Samuel Peters and Mary Ann Swartz) was born in 1852 in Pennsylvania, USA.

vi. Jane R Peters (daughter of Samuel Peters and Mary Ann Swartz) was born on March 31, 1858 in Pennsylvania, USA. She died in 1922. She married Alfred C Row. He was born in 1855 in Pennsylvania, USA.

5. vii. Mary Louisa Peters (daughter of Samuel Peters and Mary Ann Swartz) was born on March 31, 1858 in Mifflin, Dauphin County, Pennsylvania, USA[49, 51]. She died on August 3, 1924 in Home, Elizabethville, Dauphin County, Pennsylvania, USA[5, 49]. She married Thomas Edward Batdorf (son of Peter Batdorf and Elizabeth Welker) on December 6, 1874 in Rev. W.G. Engle, Dauphin County, Pennsylvania, USA[5]. He was born on July 2, 1851 in Big Run, Dauphin County, Pennsylvania, USA[49, 50]. He died on August 13, 1913 in Elizabethville, Dauphin County, Pennsylvania, USA[50].

12. **David M Wert** (son of Jacob Wert and Sarah Elizabeth Faber) was born on April 1, 1829 in Powells Valley, Dauphin County,

Pennsylvania, USA[64, 106, 107, 108]. He died on December 9, 1900 in Dayton, Dauphin County, Pennsylvania, USA[106, 107, 108, 109]. He married **Catherine Shoop** (daughter of John Shoop and Sarah Wertz) about Abt. 1849 in Dauphin County, Pennsylvania, USA.

13. **Catherine Shoop**[66] (daughter of John Shoop and Sarah Wertz) was born on February 24, 1830 in Lower Mahanoy, Northumberland County, Pennsylvania, USA[64, 107, 108, 110, 111]. She died on June 8, 1872 in Lykens, Dauphin County, Pennsylvania, USA[64, 107, 108, 110].

David M Wert was buried on December 12, 1900 in Calvary (Union) United Methodist, Wiconisco, Dauphin County, Pennsylvania, USA[106, 109, 112, 113, 114]. His cause of death was Congestion of Lungs[109]. He was counted in the census in 1830 in Halifax, Dauphin County, Pennsylvania, USA (w/father[115]). He was counted in the census in 1840 in Jackson, Dauphin, Pennsylvania (w/father[116]). He was counted in the census in 1850 in Upper Paxton, Dauphin County, Pennsylvania, USA[117]. He was counted in the census in 1860 in Lower Mahanoy Northumberland County, Pennsylvania, USA[65]. He was counted in the census in 1870 in Lykens, Dauphin County, Pennsylvania, USA[66, 110]. He was counted in the census in 1880. He was counted in the census in 1900 in Washington, Dauphin County, Pennsylvania, USA ((West)). He was employed as a Laborer in 1850[118]. He was employed as a Laborer in 1870[66, 110]. He was employed as a Laborer in 1900[106, 109]. He was affiliated with the Lutheran religion. He was affiliated with the Methodist religion.

Catherine Shoop[66] was baptized on March 6, 1830 in Zion (Stone Valley) Lutheran, Dalmatia, Northumberland County, Pennsylvania, USA[111]. She was buried in 1872 in St. Peters (Hoffman) Reformed, Loyalton, Dauphin County, Pennsylvania, USA[64, 107, 110]. She was counted in the census in 1830 in Lower Mahanoy, Northumberland County, Pennsylvania, USA (w/father). She was counted in the census in 1840 in Lower Mahanoy, Northumberland County, Pennsylvania, USA (w/father[119]). She was counted in the census in 1850 in Upper Paxtang, Dauphin County, Pennsylvania, USA[117]. She was counted in the census in 1850 in Lower Mahanoy, Northumberland County, Pennsylvania, USA[120]. She was counted in the census in 1860 in Lower Mahanoy Northumberland County, Pennsylvania, USA. She was counted in the census in 1870 in Lykens, Dauphin County, Pennsylvania, USA. She was employed as a Keeping house in 1870. Her estate was probated on June 23, 1880 in Dauphin County, Pennsylvania, USA (listed in index only)[121]. She was affiliated with the Lutheran religion. She was affiliated with the Reformed religion.

Notes for Catherine Shoop:
1850 census, Catherine is both her parent's and husband's household.

Catherine Shoop and David M Wert had the following children:

i.   Elizabeth Jane Wert (daughter of David M Wert and Catherine Shoop) was born in 1853 in Pennsylvania, USA. She married Jacob Asbury Troxell.

ii. Anna Elizabeth Wert (daughter of David M Wert and Catherine Shoop) was born in 1855 in Pennsylvania, USA. She died in 1924. She married Adam Diller Row. He was born in 1851 in Pennsylvania, USA. He died in 1929.

6.   iii. John Henry Wert (son of David M Wert and Catherine Shoop) was born on December 23, 1855 in Northumberland County, Pennsylvania, USA[60]. He died on October 30, 1924 in Harrisburg Hospital, Harrisburg, Dauphin County, Pennsylvania, USA[60]. He married Adeline Row (daughter of Daniel Row and Susan Frantz) about Abt. 1878 in Dauphin County, Pennsylvania, USA. She was born on January 2, 1860 in Dauphin County, Pennsylvania, USA[61, 62, 63]. She died on March 6, 1921 in Harrisburg, Dauphin County, Pennsylvania, USA[62].

iv. Mary Ellen Wert (daughter of David M Wert and Catherine Shoop) was born in 1859 in Pennsylvania, USA. She married John Edward Troxell.

v.   Melinda "Polly" Wert (daughter of David M Wert and Catherine Shoop) was born in 1861 in Pennsylvania, USA. She died in 1864.

vi. Martha "Mattie" Valery Wert (daughter of David M Wert and Catherine Shoop) was born in 1864 in Pennsylvania, USA. She died in 1945. She married Henry Brown. He was born in 1860.

vii. Catherine "Kate" Ann Wert (daughter of David M Wert and Catherine Shoop) was born in 1866 in Pennsylvania, USA. She died in 1917. She married John Copp. He was born in 1860.

viii. Amelia Ida Wert (daughter of David M Wert and Catherine Shoop) was born in 1868 in Pennsylvania, USA. She married Isaac Smith. He was born in 1860.

ix. Daniel Monroe Wert (son of David M Wert and Catherine Shoop) was born in 1870 in Pennsylvania, USA. He married Emma ?. She was born in 1870 in Pennsylvania, USA. He married Susan ?. She was born in 1880.

x. Isaac Franklin Wert (son of David M Wert and Catherine Shoop) was born in 1871 in Pennsylvania, USA. He married Catherine "Kate" M Carl. She was born in 1873 in Pennsylvania, USA.

14. **Daniel Row** (son of John William Rowe and Barbara Rudy) was born on July 10, 1813 in Lykens, Dauphin County, Pennsylvania, USA[62, 122, 123, 124]. He died on July 31, 1871 in Berrysburg, Dauphin County, Pennsylvania, USA[123, 124]. He married **Susan Frantz** (daughter of Adam Frantz and Susan Gieseman) about Abt. 1840 in Dauphin County, Pennsylvania, USA.

15. **Susan Frantz** (daughter of Adam Frantz and Susan Gieseman) was born on March 23, 1819 in Mifflin, Dauphin County, Pennsylvania, USA[62, 123, 125]. She died on October 17, 1861 in Berrysburg, Dauphin County, Pennsylvania, USA[123, 125].

Daniel Row was baptized on August 14, 1813 in St. Johns (Hill) Lutheran, Berrysburg, Dauphin County, Pennsylvania, USA[122, 123]. He was buried in July 1871 in St. Johns (Hill) Lutheran, Berrysburg,

Dauphin County, Pennsylvania, USA[124]. His cause of death was Bright's disease (ie, Chronic inflammation of kidneys)[123]. He was counted in the census in 1820 in Mifflin, Dauphin County, Pennsylvania, USA (w/father[126]). He was counted in the census in 1830 in Halifax, Dauphin County, Pennsylvania, USA (w/father[127]). He was counted in the census in 1840 in Wiconisco, Dauphin County, Pennsylvania, USA[128, 129]. He was counted in the census in 1850 in Washington, Dauphin County, Pennsylvania, USA[130]. He was counted in the census in 1860 in Washington, Dauphin County, Pennsylvania, USA[72, 131]. He was counted in the census in 1870 in Wiconisco, Dauphin County, Pennsylvania, USA[132]. He was employed as a Laborer between 1850-1870[72, 130, 131, 132]. His estate was probated on August 28, 1871 in Dauphin County, Pennsylvania, USA(listed in index only)[133]. He was affiliated with the Lutheran religion.

Susan Frantz was buried in 1861 in St. Johns (Hill) Lutheran, Berrysburg, Dauphin County, Pennsylvania, USA[134]. She was counted in the census in 1820 in Mifflin, Dauphin County, Pennsylvania, USA (w/father[135]). She was counted in the census in 1830. She was counted in the census in 1840 in Wiconisco, Dauphin County, Pennsylvania, USA (w/husband). She was counted in the census in 1850 in Washington, Dauphin County, Pennsylvania, USA. She was counted in the census in 1860 in Washington, Dauphin County, Pennsylvania, USA. She was employed as a Homemaker. She was affiliated with the Lutheran religion.

Notes for Susan Frantz:
Susan was named after her mother "Susan" Gieseman.

Susan Frantz and Daniel Row had the following children:
   i.   Sarah Ann Row (daughter of Daniel Row and Susan Frantz) was born in 1841 in Pennsylvania, USA. She died in 1859[74].

   ii. Angelina Row (daughter of Daniel Row and Susan Frantz) was born in 1843 in Pennsylvania, USA. She died in 1936[74]. She married Jacob Zerby. He was born in 1840 in

Pennsylvania, USA. He died in 1913[74].

iii. Adam Diller Row (son of Daniel Row and Susan Frantz) was born in 1851 in Pennsylvania, USA. He died in 1929. He married Anna Elizabeth Wert. She was born in 1855 in Pennsylvania, USA. She died in 1924.

iv. Susan Row (daughter of Daniel Row and Susan Frantz) was born in 1852 in Pennsylvania, USA. She died in 1933. She married William Henry Keiper. He was born in 1851 in Pennsylvania, USA. He died in 1913[74].

v. Amelia Row (daughter of Daniel Row and Susan Frantz) was born in 1854 in Pennsylvania, USA. She married Isaac F Chubb. He was born in 1849 in Pennsylvania, USA.

vi. Leah Jane Row (daughter of Daniel Row and Susan Frantz) was born in 1857 in Pennsylvania, USA. She married ? Michael.

7.   vii. Adeline Row (daughter of Daniel Row and Susan Frantz) was born on January 2, 1860 in Dauphin County, Pennsylvania, USA[61, 62, 63]. She died on March 6, 1921 in Harrisburg, Dauphin County, Pennsylvania, USA[62]. She married John Henry Wert (son of David M Wert and Catherine Shoop) about Abt. 1878 in Dauphin County, Pennsylvania, USA. He was born on December 23, 1855 in Northumberland County, Pennsylvania, USA[60]. He died on October 30, 1924 in Harrisburg Hospital, Harrisburg, Dauphin County, Pennsylvania, USA[60].

Generation 5

16. **Jacob Peter Batdorf** (son of George Peter Batdorf and Barbara Weiss) was born about Abt. 1793 in Pennsylvania, USA. He died in 1829 in Dauphin County, Pennsylvania, USA[76]. He married **Maria Catherine Steiner** (daughter of George? Steiner and Elizabeth ?) on February 20, 1813 in Christ Lutheran, Stouchsburg, Berks County, Pennsylvania, USA.

17. **Maria Catherine Steiner** (daughter of George? Steiner and Elizabeth

?) was born in 1792 in Berks County, Pennsylvania, USA[136]. She died between 1830-1840 in Dauphin County, Pennsylvania, USA.

Jacob Peter Batdorf was buried in 1829 in Loyalton, Dauphin County, Pennsylvania, USA. He was counted in the census in 1800 in Heidelberg, Dauphin County, Pennsylvania, USA (w/father[137]). He was counted in the census in 1810. He was counted in the census in 1820 in Lykens, Dauphin County, Pennsylvania, USA[138, 139]. He was employed as a Farmer in 1820. His estate was probated in 1829 in Dauphin County, Pennsylvania, USA(listed in index only)[140]. He was affiliated with the Lutheran religion. He lived in Berrysburg, Dauphin County, Pennsylvania, USA between 1815-1828[141].

Notes for Jacob Peter Batdorf:
More research needs done here. Many inconsistencies. It seems at this point most probable that this Peter and wife Catherine have been confused with his parents, Peter and Catherine. It seems there may have been a skipped generation in most data I have seen [author, 2000]

Maria Catherine Steiner was counted in the census in 1820 in Lykens, Dauphin County, Pennsylvania, USA (w/husband[142]). She was counted in the census in 1830 in Lykens, Dauphin County, Pennsylvania, USA[142, 143, 144]. She was affiliated with the Lutheran religion. She lived in Dauphin County, Pennsylvania, USA between 1832-1833[76].

Maria Catherine Steiner and Jacob Peter Batdorf had the following children:
8.   i.   Peter Batdorf (son of Jacob Peter Batdorf and Maria Catherine Steiner) was born on January 20, 1814 in Lykens, Dauphin County, Pennsylvania, USA[49, 75, 76, 77, 78]. He died on December 5, 1880 in Lykens, Dauphin County, Pennsylvania, USA[49, 75, 76, 77, 78, 79, 80]. He married Elizabeth Welker (daughter of John Welker and Maria Elizabeth Messerschmidt) about Abt. 1831 in Dauphin County, Pennsylvania, USA. She was born on November 23, 1812

in Lykens, Dauphin County, Pennsylvania, USA[49, 75, 76]. She died on July 7, 1868 in Lykens, Dauphin County, Pennsylvania, USA[49, 75, 76, 81]. He married Magdalena "Mollie" Lettich about Abt. 1870. She was born in 1829. She died in 1891[48].

ii. Sarah Batdorf (daughter of Jacob Peter Batdorf and Maria Catherine Steiner) was born in 1815 in Pennsylvania, USA.

iii. John Batdorf (son of Jacob Peter Batdorf and Maria Catherine Steiner) was born in 1817 in Pennsylvania, USA.

iv. Catherine Batdorf (daughter of Jacob Peter Batdorf and Maria Catherine Steiner) was born in 1818 in Pennsylvania, USA.

v. Thomas Batdorf (son of Jacob Peter Batdorf and Maria Catherine Steiner) was born in 1820 in Pennsylvania, USA. He married Magdalena "Maddie" ?. She was born in 1823 in Pennsylvania, USA.

vi. Jonathan Batdorf (son of Jacob Peter Batdorf and Maria Catherine Steiner) was born in 1822 in Pennsylvania, USA.

vii. Daniel Batdorf (son of Jacob Peter Batdorf and Maria Catherine Steiner) was born in 1824 in Pennsylvania, USA. He married Christina Zimmerman. She was born in 1826 in Pennsylvania, USA.

viii. Jacob Batdorf (son of Jacob Peter Batdorf and Maria Catherine Steiner) was born in 1826 in Pennsylvania, USA. He married Rosanna ?. She was born in 1828 in Pennsylvania, USA.

ix. Elizabeth Batdorf (daughter of Jacob Peter Batdorf and Maria Catherine Steiner) was born in 1828 in Pennsylvania, USA.

18. **John Welker** (son of Valentine Welker and Susan Jury) was born on August 10, 1783 in Millersburg, Lancaster (Dauphin) County, Pennsylvania, USA[145, 146]. He died on November 11, 1854 in Gratz, Dauphin County, Pennsylvania, USA[75, 147, 148]. He married **Maria Elizabeth Messerschmidt** (daughter of Andrew Messerschmidt and Eva Schrot) about Abt. 1806 in Dauphin County, Pennsylvania, USA.

19. **Maria Elizabeth Messerschmidt** (daughter of Andrew Messerschmidt and Eva Schrot) was born in January 1780 in Elizabethville, Lancaster (Dauphin) County, Pennsylvania, USA[149, 150, 151]. She died in 1850 in Gratz, Dauphin County, Pennsylvania, USA[150].

John Welker was baptized on September 22, 1783 in Old Salem (Werts) Lutheran, Millersburg, Lancaster (Dauphin) County, Pennsylvania, USA[146]. He was buried in 1854 in Simeon Union, Gratz, Dauphin County, Pennsylvania, USA[75, 149, 152]. His cause of death was Influenza[149, 152]. He was counted in the census in 1790 in Dauphin County, Pennsylvania, USA (w/father[153]). He was counted in the census in 1800 in Upper Paxton, Dauphin County, Pennsylvania, USA (w/father[154]). He was counted in the census in 1810 in Northern Dauphin County, Pennsylvania, USA[155]. He was counted in the census in 1820 in Lykens, Dauphin County, Pennsylvania, USA[89, 156]. He was counted in the census in 1830 in Lykens, Dauphin County, Pennsylvania, USA[90, 157]. He was counted in the census in 1840 in Lykens, Dauphin County, Pennsylvania, USA[158, 159]. He was counted in the census in 1850 in Lykens, Dauphin County, Pennsylvania, USA[160]. He was employed as a Manufacturing in 1820[89]. He was employed as a Weaver in 1843[149, 152]. He was employed as a Laborer in 1850[160]. His estate was probated in 1854 in Dauphin County, Pennsylvania, USA(listed in index only)[161]. He was affiliated with the Lutheran religion. He was affiliated with the Union (Lutheran) religion.

Notes for John Welker:
On several occasions, beginning in 1819, John Welker's name appears in the account book of Leonard Reedy. Weaver shuttles and other items were purchased frequently by George and John Welker under the same account. In February 1832, Leonard Ready

acknowledged the deed transferring a house from Simon Gratz to John Welker. A charge of twelve and one half cents was noted in Reedy's account book. Over the years the Welkers did weaving, grubbing, and hauling for Reedy, at fifty cents per day in exchange for his services. Mr. Welker penned a Will before his death. He states that he wants his body

to be buried in the graveyard at the Lutheran and German Reformed Church on the side of the new Church. He also wanted the rites of the new Church for his funeral. In his Will John mentioned daughter Hannah, married to George Hoffman, and henamed his son Joseph executor of his Will. On February 20. 1832, Simon Gratz sold Lot 85 to John Welker for $43.95. John Welker was already living in Gratz at that time. John Welker owned this property for many years. A log house was built on the lot as early as 1834. By 1843 a barn was added and John Welker, occupant, was trading as a weaver. The 1850 census shows John Welker and his wife Elizabeth living in part of this house. Isaac Schoffstall, age 21, and his wife Sarah, along with William, his young son, also lived on this Lot in separate quarters. John Welker helped establish Samuel's Lutheran and Reformed Church on Loat 18. He and John Kissinger served as the trustee's to whom George Hoffman sold that vacant lot in 1846. [Roger Cramer, RogerCubs@aol.com]

Maria Elizabeth Messerschmidt was buried in 1850. She was counted in the census in 1790. She was counted in the census in 1800 in Upper Paxton, Dauphin County, Pennsylvania, USA (w/father[162]). She was counted in the census in 1810 in Northern Dauphin County, Pennsylvania, USA (w/husband). She was counted in the census in 1820 in Lykens, Dauphin County, Pennsylvania, USA (w/husband). She was counted in the census in 1830 in Lykens, Dauphin County, Pennsylvania, USA (w/husband). She was counted in the census in 1840 in Lykens, Dauphin County, Pennsylvania, USA (w/husband). She was counted in the census in 1850 in Lykens, Dauphin County, Pennsylvania, USA.

Maria Elizabeth Messerschmidt and John Welker had the following children:

i. George Welker (son of John Welker and Maria Elizabeth Messerschmidt) was born in 1807 in Dauphin County, Pennsylvania, USA. He died in 1889. He married Catherine ?. She was born in 1805 in Pennsylvania, USA.

ii. Rachel Welker (daughter of John Welker and Maria Elizabeth Messerschmidt) was born in 1809 in Dauphin County, Pennsylvania, USA. She married Jacob Martz. He was born in 1800.

iii. ? Welker (daughter of John Welker and Maria Elizabeth Messerschmidt) was born about Abt. 1811 in Pennsylvania, USA.

9. iv. Elizabeth Welker (daughter of John Welker and Maria Elizabeth Messerschmidt) was born on November 23, 1812 in Lykens, Dauphin County, Pennsylvania, USA[49, 75, 76]. She died on July 7, 1868 in Lykens, Dauphin County, Pennsylvania, USA[49, 75, 76, 81]. She married Peter Batdorf (son of Jacob Peter Batdorf and Maria Catherine Steiner) about Abt. 1831 in Dauphin County, Pennsylvania, USA. He was born on January 20, 1814 in Lykens, Dauphin County, Pennsylvania, USA[49, 75, 76, 77, 78]. He died on December 5, 1880 in Lykens, Dauphin County, Pennsylvania, USA[49, 75, 76, 77, 78, 79, 80].

v. William Henry Welker (son of John Welker and Maria Elizabeth Messerschmidt) was born in 1814 in Pennsylvania, USA. He married Anna ?. She was born in 1810 in Pennsylvania, USA.

vi. David Welker (son of John Welker and Maria Elizabeth Messerschmidt) was born in 1815 in Dauphin County, Pennsylvania, USA.

vii. Anna Welker (daughter of John Welker and Maria Elizabeth Messerschmidt) was born in 1817 in Dauphin County, Pennsylvania, USA.

viii. Sarah Welker (daughter of John Welker and Maria Elizabeth Messerschmidt) was born in 1818 in Dauphin

County, Pennsylvania, USA.

    ix.   Joseph Welker (son of John Welker and Maria Elizabeth Messerschmidt) was born in 1820 in Dauphin County, Pennsylvania, USA. He married Susan ?. She was born in 1823 in Pennsylvania, USA.

20.   **John Peters** (son of John Peters and ?) was born about Abt. 1791 in Pennsylvania, USA[163]. He died about Abt. 1840 in Buffalo, Union County, Pennsylvania, USA[163]. He married **Anna Maria ?** (daughter of ? and ?) about Abt. 1820 in Union County, Pennsylvania, USA[163].

21.   **Anna Maria ?** (daughter of ? and ?) was born about Abt. 1792 in Pennsylvania, USA[163, 164]. She died on October 22, 1852 in East Buffalo, Union County, Pennsylvania, USA[165].

John Peters was counted in the census in 1800 in East Buffalo, Northumberland (Union), Pennsylvania, USA (w/father[166]). He was counted in the census in 1810 in East Buffalo, Northumberland County, Pennsylvania, USA (w/father[167]). He was counted in the census in 1820 in Buffalo, Union County, Pennsylvania, USA (w/father[168]). He was counted in the census in 1830 in Buffalo, Union County, Pennsylvania, USA[95, 169]. He lived in East Buffalo, Union County, Pennsylvania, USA about Abt. 1830[170].

Anna Maria ? was counted in the census in 1800. She was counted in the census in 1810. She was counted in the census in 1820. She was counted in the census in 1830 in Buffalo, Union County, Pennsylvania, USA[169]. She was counted in the census in 1840 in Buffalo, Union County, Pennsylvania, USA (w/father-in-law). She was counted in the census in 1850 in East Buffalo, Union County, Pennsylvania, USA[164].

Anna Maria ? and John Peters had the following children:
  10.   i.   Samuel Peters (son of John Peters and Anna Maria ?) was born in 1821 in Buffalo, Union County, Pennsylvania, USA. He died between 1860-1870 in Perry County, Pennsylvania, USA. He married Mary Ann Swartz

(daughter of John Swartz and Anna ?) about Abt. 1840 in Union County, Pennsylvania, USA. She was born on January 5, 1820 in Juniata, Perry County, Pennsylvania, USA[92]. She died on August 9, 1897 in Washington, Dauphin County, Pennsylvania, USA[93, 94].

ii. Andrew J Peters (son of John Peters and Anna Maria ?) was born about Abt. 1822 in Pennsylvania, USA. He died between 1870-1880. He married Sarah J Bird?. She was born about Abt. 1825 in Pennsylvania, USA.

iii. Jonathan Peters (son of John Peters and Anna Maria ?) was born about Abt. 1825 in Pennsylvania, USA. He died before Bef. 1850.

iv. Elias Peters (son of John Peters and Anna Maria ?) was born in April 1829 in Pennsylvania, USA. He died between 1870-1880. He married Angelina ?. She was born in March 1835 in Pennsylvania, USA.

v. Matilda Peters (daughter of John Peters and Anna Maria ?) was born about Abt. 1837 in Pennsylvania, USA.

22. **John Swartz** (son of John Swartz and Mary ?) was born about Abt. 1780 in Pennsylvania, USA. He died between 1840-1850 in Pennsylvania, USA. He married **Anna ?** (daughter of ? and ?) about Abt. 1815 in Perry County, Pennsylvania, USA.

23. **Anna ?** (daughter of ? and ?) was born about Abt. 1785 in Pennsylvania, USA. She died after Aft. 1840 in Perry County, Pennsylvania, USA.

John Swartz was counted in the census in 1800. He was counted in the census in 1810. He was counted in the census in 1820 in Juniata, Perry County, Pennsylvania, USA[100, 171]. He was counted in the census in 1830 in Juniata, Perry County, Pennsylvania, USA[102]. He was counted in the census in 1840 in Juniata, Perry County, Pennsylvania, USA[172].

Anna ? was counted in the census in 1800. She was counted in the census in 1810. She was counted in the census in 1820 in Juniata, Perry County, Pennsylvania, USA (w/husband). She was counted in the census in 1830 in Juniata, Perry County, Pennsylvania, USA (w/husband[102]). She was counted in the census in 1840 in Juniata, Perry County, Pennsylvania, USA (w/husband[172]).

Anna ? and John Swartz had the following children:

11. i. Mary Ann Swartz (daughter of John Swartz and Anna ?) was born on January 5, 1820 in Juniata, Perry County, Pennsylvania, USA[92]. She died on August 9, 1897 in Washington, Dauphin County, Pennsylvania, USA[93, 94]. She married Samuel Peters (son of John Peters and Anna Maria ?) about Abt. 1840 in Union County, Pennsylvania, USA. He was born in 1821 in Buffalo, Union County, Pennsylvania, USA. He died between 1860-1870 in Perry County, Pennsylvania, USA.

ii. George? Swartz (son of John Swartz and Anna ?) was born about Abt. 1821 in Pennsylvania, USA. He died between 1900-1910.

iii. John Swartz (son of John Swartz and Anna ?) was born about Abt. 1825 in Pennsylvania, USA. He died between 1870-1880.

24. **Jacob Wert** (son of John Jacob Wirth and Anna Sophia Susan Miller) was born on July 20, 1804 in Lykens, Dauphin County, Pennsylvania, USA[64, 108]. He died in 1890 in Halifax, Dauphin County, Pennsylvania, USA[108, 173]. He married **Sarah Elizabeth Faber** (daughter of John Faber and Maria "Mollie" Magdalena Rudy) about Abt. 1828 in Dauphin County, Pennsylvania, USA[64].

25. **Sarah Elizabeth Faber** (daughter of John Faber and Maria "Mollie" Magdalena Rudy) was born on May 25, 1807 in Lancaster (Lebanon) County, Pennsylvania, USA[64, 108]. She died on April 5, 1902 in Dauphin County, Pennsylvania, USA[64, 174].

Jacob Wert was buried in 1890 in St. Peters (Fetterhoff) Union, Halifax, Dauphin County, Pennsylvania, USA[64]. He was buried in St.

Pauls (Bowermans) Lutheran, Enterline, Dauphin County, Pennsylvania, USA[175]. He was counted in the census in 1810 in Upper Paxton, Dauphin County, Pennsylvania, USA (w/father[176]). He was counted in the census in 1820 in Upper Paxton, Dauphin County, Pennsylvania, USA (w/father[177]). He was counted in the census in 1830 in Halifax, Dauphin County, Pennsylvania, USA[178, 179]. He was counted in the census in 1840 in Jackson, Dauphin, Pennsylvania[116, 180]. He was counted in the census in 1850 in Jackson, Dauphin County, Pennsylvania, USA[117]. He was counted in the census in 1860 in Halifax, Dauphin County, Pennsylvania, USA ((Wist)[181]). He was counted in the census in 1870 in Slatington, Lehigh County, Pennsylvania, USA[182]. He was counted in the census in 1880. He was employed as a Farmer in 1850[117]. He was employed as a Laborer in 1860[181]. He was employed as a Works on RR in 1870[183]. He was affiliated with the Lutheran religion. He was affiliated with the Lutheran (Union) religion.

Sarah Elizabeth Faber was buried in 1902 in St. Pauls (Bowermans) Lutheran, Enterline, Dauphin County, Pennsylvania, USA[174, 184]. She was buried in 1902 in St. Peters (Fetterhoff) Union, Halifax, Dauphin County, Pennsylvania, USA[185]. She was counted in the census in 1810 in Upper Paxton, Dauphin County, Pennsylvania, USA (w/father[186]). She was counted in the census in 1820 in Upper Paxton, Dauphin County, Pennsylvania, USA (w/father[187]). She was counted in the census in 1830 in Halifax, Dauphin County, Pennsylvania, USA. She was counted in the census in 1840 in Jackson, Dauphin, Pennsylvania (w/husband). She was counted in the census in 1850 in Jackson, Dauphin County, Pennsylvania, USA. She was counted in the census in 1860 in Halifax, Dauphin County, Pennsylvania, USA. She was counted in the census in 1870 in Upper Paxton, Dauphin County, Pennsylvania, USA[188]. She was counted in the census in 1880. She was counted in the census in 1900. She was employed as a Domestic in 1870[189]. She was employed as a Keeping house in 1870[183]. She was affiliated with the Lutheran religion. She was affiliated with the Lutheran (Union) religion.

Sarah Elizabeth Faber and Jacob Wert had the following children:

12.　i.　David M Wert (son of Jacob Wert and Sarah Elizabeth Faber) was born on April 1, 1829 in Powells Valley,

Dauphin County, Pennsylvania, USA[64, 106, 107, 108]. He died on December 9, 1900 in Dayton, Dauphin County, Pennsylvania, USA[106, 107, 108, 109]. He married Catherine Shoop (daughter of John Shoop and Sarah Wertz) about Abt. 1849 in Dauphin County, Pennsylvania, USA. She was born on February 24, 1830 in Lower Mahanoy, Northumberland County, Pennsylvania, USA[64, 107, 108, 110, 111]. She died on June 8, 1872 in Lykens, Dauphin County, Pennsylvania, USA[64, 107, 108, 110]. He married Elizabeth Bellis about Abt. 1875. She was born in 1843 in Pennsylvania, USA.

ii. Elizabeth Wert (daughter of Jacob Wert and Sarah Elizabeth Faber) was born in 1833 in Pennsylvania, USA.

iii. Catherine Wert (daughter of Jacob Wert and Sarah Elizabeth Faber) was born in 1835 in Pennsylvania, USA.

iv. Sarah Wert (daughter of Jacob Wert and Sarah Elizabeth Faber) was born in 1835 in Pennsylvania, USA.

v. John Henry Wert (son of Jacob Wert and Sarah Elizabeth Faber) was born in 1837 in Pennsylvania, USA. He married Mary Margaret Pinkerton. She was born in 1841 in Pennsylvania, USA.

vi. Adam Washington Wert (son of Jacob Wert and Sarah Elizabeth Faber) was born in 1841 in Pennsylvania, USA. He married Sarah Elizabeth Faber. She was born in 1846 in Pennsylvania, USA.

vii. Peter Martin Wert (son of Jacob Wert and Sarah Elizabeth Faber) was born in 1843 in Dauphin County, Pennsylvania, USA.

viii. Matthew Wert (son of Jacob Wert and Sarah Elizabeth Faber) was born in 1847 in Pennsylvania, USA.

ix. Martha Wert (daughter of Jacob Wert and Sarah Elizabeth Faber) was born in 1848 in Pennsylvania, USA.

26. **John Shoop** (son of John George Schupp and Anna Margaret Miller) was born on August 1, 1805 in Dauphin Co., ,Pennsylvania, USA[112, 190, 191]. He died on December 13, 1858 in Lower Mahanoy, Northumberland County, Pennsylvania, USA[112, 191, 192]. He married **Sarah Wertz** (daughter of John Wertz and Joanna Catherine Garman) about Abt. 1826 in Northumberland County, Pennsylvania, USA.

27. **Sarah Wertz** (daughter of John Wertz and Joanna Catherine Garman) was born on January 18, 1811 in Northumberland County, Pennsylvania, USA[110, 112, 193]. She died in 1847 in Lower Mahanoy, Northumberland County, Pennsylvania, USA[193].

John Shoop was baptized on August 8, 1805 in St. Davids (Salem) Reformed, Millersburg, Dauphin County, Pennsylvania, USA. He was buried in 1858 in Zion (Stone Valley) Lutheran, Dalmatia, Northumberland County, Pennsylvania, USA. He was counted in the census in 1810 in Upper Paxton, Dauphin County, Pennsylvania, USA (w/father[194]). He was counted in the census in 1820 in Upper Paxton, Dauphin County, Pennsylvania, USA (w/father[195]). He was counted in the census in 1830 in Lower Mahanoy, Northumberland County, Pennsylvania, USA[196]. He was counted in the census in 1840 in Lower Mahanoy, Northumberland County, Pennsylvania, USA. He was counted in the census in 1850 in Lower Mahanoy, Northumberland, Pennsylvania, USA(Joyn)[197]. He was employed as a Farmer in 1850[197]. His estate was probated on December 23, 1858 in Lower Mahanoy, Northumberland County, Pennsylvania, USA[198]. He was affiliated with the Lutheran religion. He was affiliated with the Reformed religion.

Sarah Wertz was buried about Abt. 1847 in Zion (Stone Valley) Lutheran, Dalmatia, Northumberland County, Pennsylvania, USA. She was counted in the census in 1820 in Lower Mahanoy, Northumberland County, Pennsylvania, USA (w/father[199]). She was counted in the census in 1830 in Lower Mahanoy, Northumberland County, Pennsylvania, USA (w/husband). She was counted in the census in 1840 in Lower Mahanoy, Northumberland County, Pennsylvania, USA (w/husband). She was employed as a

Homemaker about Abt. 1835. She was affiliated with the Lutheran religion.

Sarah Wertz and John Shoop had the following children:

i. Anna Shoop (daughter of John Shoop and Sarah Wertz) was born in 1827 in Pennsylvania, USA.

13. ii. Catherine Shoop[66] (daughter of John Shoop and Sarah Wertz) was born on February 24, 1830 in Lower Mahanoy, Northumberland County, Pennsylvania, USA[64, 107, 108, 110, 111]. She died on June 8, 1872 in Lykens, Dauphin County, Pennsylvania, USA[64, 107, 108, 110]. She married David M Wert (son of Jacob Wert and Sarah Elizabeth Faber) about Abt. 1849 in Dauphin County, Pennsylvania, USA. He was born on April 1, 1829 in Powells Valley, Dauphin County, Pennsylvania, USA[64, 106, 107, 108]. He died on December 9, 1900 in Dayton, Dauphin County, Pennsylvania, USA[106, 107, 108, 109].

iii. Anna Maria Shoop (daughter of John Shoop and Sarah Wertz) was born in 1831 in Pennsylvania, USA. She married Jeremiah Crawford. He was born in 1833.

iv. Elizabeth Shoop (daughter of John Shoop and Sarah Wertz) was born in 1833 in Dauphin County, Pennsylvania, USA. She married William Henry Welker. He was born in 1835.

v. Salome "Sarah" Shoop (daughter of John Shoop and Sarah Wertz) was born in 1841 in Pennsylvania, USA. She married Simon Tschopp. He was born in 1833.

28. **John William Rowe** (son of Francis "Frank" Rowe and Maria Catherine Traut) was born in June 1785 in Strasburg, Lancaster County, Pennsylvania, USA[200, 201, 202, 203]. He died in 1877 in Berrysburg, Dauphin County, Pennsylvania, USA[200, 202]. He married **Barbara Rudy** (daughter of Jacob Rudy and Susan Jungblut) in 1810 in Strasburg, Lancaster County, Pennsylvania, USA[123, 202].

29. **Barbara Rudy** (daughter of Jacob Rudy and Susan Jungblut) was born on April 11, 1796 in Strasburg, Lancaster County, Pennsylvania,

USA[201, 204]. She died on December 15, 1881 in Berrysburg, Dauphin County, Pennsylvania, USA[123, 201, 204].

John William Rowe was buried in 1877 in St. Johns (Hill) Lutheran, Berrysburg, Dauphin County, Pennsylvania, USA[123, 204, 205]. He was counted in the census in 1790 in Strasburg, Lancaster County, Pennsylvania, USA (w/father[206]). He was counted in the census in 1800 in Strasburg, Lancaster County, Pennsylvania, USA (w/father[207]). He was counted in the census in 1810. He was counted in the census in 1820 in Mifflin, Dauphin County, Pennsylvania, USA ((Rosie)[208, 209]). He was counted in the census in 1830 in Halifax, Dauphin County, Pennsylvania, USA[210, 211]. He was counted in the census in 1840 in Wiconisco, Dauphin County, Pennsylvania, USA[212]. He was counted in the census in 1850 in Wiconisco, Dauphin County, Pennsylvania, USA[213]. He was counted in the census in 1860 in Wiconisco, Dauphin County, Pennsylvania, USA[131]. He was counted in the census in 1870 in Washington, Dauphin County, Pennsylvania, USA[214]. He was employed as a Agriculture in 1820[215]. He was employed as a Carpenter about Abt. 1840. He was employed as a Laborer between 1850-1870[131, 214, 216]. He was affiliated with the Lutheran[217] religion. He lived in Berrysburg, Dauphin County, Pennsylvania, USA between 1812-1820[146]. He signed his will on April 3, 1873 in Dauphin County, Pennsylvania, USA(listed in index)[218].

Notes for John William Rowe:
Ancestor of Jonas Row farmer and justice of the peace, was born in Mifflin township, now Washington Township, Dauphin county, Pa., May 11, 1839. He owned, improved and worked a farm of ninety acres in Washington township in connection with which he carried on a butchering business, also a store at Matterstown. Mr. Row first held Democratic views in politics, but changed for a time to the Republican party, and finally returned to the Democratic party. He has served as supervisor of roads, tax collector, and in other offices. He died in Schuylkill County at the age of eighty-two. Mr. Row was well known and highly respected. He was comfortably cared for in his declining years by his faithful son, Jonas. He was a member of the old school Lutheran church, in which he was deacon and trustee, also Sunday-school superintendent and teacher. Jonas Row attended the

schools of Washington Township in the winter, and worked with his father in the various departments of his business until he was twenty-one years of age. On reaching his majority he was employed by his father on wages. He worked two years on the homestead farm, at Matterstown, and two years in Lykens Valley, at butchering, etc. In 1863 Mr. Row enlisted, at Harrisburg, in the One Hundred and Twenty-seventh regiment, Pennsylvania volunteers, under Colonel Jennings and Captain Bell. He participated in the battle of Gettysburg, and was wounded in the knee, the result of which was to lame him fur life. He was discharged at the end of three months' service, but re-enlisted in the fall of 1863, in company F, Sixteenth Pennsylvania cavalry, under Colonel Robinson and Capt. J. H. Ressler. He was at Petersburg five days, and on account of bravery in action was promoted to the rank of orderly to General Gregg. Mr. Row was at the surrender of General Lee, and was mustered out of service in 1865. He returned home and engaged in trading in Lykens Valley for two years, after which he bought thirty-three acres of land and added twenty-two acres more, in Washington Township. This farm he improved at an expense of $5,000. But Mr. Row became security for a friend, through which he sustained a loss of $4000, and was forced to sell his farm which brought only $5,000. In 1890 he removed to Jefferson Township and purchased eighty acres, the buildings on which he remodeled and enlarged, and fitted the place for farming and stock raising. [Dauphin County, Pennsylvania Genealogy Transcription Project, http://maley.net/transcription/]

Barbara Rudy was buried in 1881 in St. Johns (Hill) Lutheran, Berrysburg, Dauphin County, Pennsylvania, USA[123, 219]. She was counted in the census in 1800 in Lancaster County, Pennsylvania, USA (w/father[220]). She was counted in the census in 1810. She was counted in the census in 1820 in Mifflin, Dauphin County, Pennsylvania, USA (w/husband). She was counted in the census in 1830 in Halifax, Dauphin County, Pennsylvania, USA (w/husband). She was counted in the census in 1840 in Wiconisco, Dauphin County, Pennsylvania, USA (w/husband). She was counted in the census in 1850 in Wiconisco, Dauphin County, Pennsylvania, USA. She was counted in the census in 1860 in Wiconisco, Dauphin County, Pennsylvania, USA. She was counted in the census in 1870 in Washington, Dauphin County, Pennsylvania, USA[214]. She was counted in the census in 1880 in Washington, Dauphin County, Pennsylvania, USA (w/son Jacob[221]). She was employed as a Keeping house in 1870[214]. She was employed as a Lady in 1880[221]. She was affiliated with the Lutheran religion.

Barbara Rudy and John William Rowe had the following children:

    i.   Wendel Row (son of John William Rowe and Barbara Rudy) was born in 1811 in Pennsylvania, USA. He married Rachel ?. She was born in 1813 in Pennsylvania, USA.

    ii.   Jacob Row (son of John William Rowe and Barbara Rudy) was born in 1812 in Dauphin County, Pennsylvania, USA. He married Susan Matter. She was born in 1820 in Pennsylvania, USA.

14.   iii.   Daniel Row (son of John William Rowe and Barbara Rudy) was born on July 10, 1813 in Lykens, Dauphin County, Pennsylvania, USA[62, 122, 123, 124]. He died on July 31, 1871 in Berrysburg, Dauphin County, Pennsylvania, USA[123, 124]. He married Susan Frantz (daughter of Adam Frantz and Susan Gieseman) about Abt. 1840 in Dauphin County, Pennsylvania, USA. She was born on March 23, 1819 in Mifflin, Dauphin County, Pennsylvania, USA[62, 123, 125]. She died on October 17, 1861 in Berrysburg, Dauphin County, Pennsylvania, USA[123, 125].

    iv.   Susan Row (daughter of John William Rowe and Barbara Rudy) was born in 1815 in Pennsylvania, USA.

    v.   John Row (son of John William Rowe and Barbara Rudy) was born in 1817 in Pennsylvania, USA. He married Matilda ?. She was born in 1821 in Pennsylvania, USA.

    vi.   Elizabeth Row (daughter of John William Rowe and Barbara Rudy) was born in 1819 in Pennsylvania, USA.

    vii.   Sarah Row (daughter of John William Rowe and Barbara Rudy) was born in 1820 in Pennsylvania, USA.

    viii.   Joseph Row (son of John William Rowe and Barbara Rudy) was born in 1828 in Pennsylvania, USA. He married

Catherine ?. She was born in 1833 in Pennsylvania, USA.

30. **Adam Frantz** (son of William Frantz and Anna Margaret Gieseman) was born in 1780 in Lykens, Lancaster (Dauphin) County, Pennsylvania, USA[222, 223]. He died between 1825-1830 in Dauphin County, Pennsylvania, USA. He married **Susan Gieseman** (daughter of John William Gieseman and Anna Margaret Gruber) on October 6, 1811 in Upper Paxton, Dauphin County, Pennsylvania, USA[224, 225, 226].

31. **Susan Gieseman** (daughter of John William Gieseman and Anna Margaret Gruber) was born on November 10, 1787 in Tulpehocken, Berks County, Pennsylvania, USA[224, 227]. She died on February 15, 1826 in Mifflin, Dauphin County, Pennsylvania, USA[224, 227, 228].

Adam Frantz was baptized about Abt. 1785 in St. Johns (Hill) Lutheran, Berrysburg, Dauphin County, Pennsylvania, USA. He was counted in the census in 1790 in Strasburg, Lancaster County, Pennsylvania, USA (w/father[229]). He was counted in the census in 1800 in Upper Paxton, Dauphin County, Pennsylvania, USA (w/father[230]). He was counted in the census in 1810. He was counted in the census in 1820 in Mifflin, Dauphin County, Pennsylvania, USA[231]. He was confirmed between 1816-1819 (St. Peters (Hoffmans) Union, Lykens, Dauphin County, Pennsylvania, USA[232]). He served in the military between September 2, 1814-March 5, 1815 (War of 1812, Private, 2nd Reg Pennsylvania, USA Militia (Ritschers), 1st Brig (York, Capt. Philip Fetterhoff)[233]). He was employed as a Manufacturing in 1820[234]. He was affiliated with the Lutheran religion. He was affiliated with the Reformed religion.

Susan Gieseman was baptized on May 30, 1788 in Pennsylvania, USA[228]. She was buried on February 17, 1826 in St. Johns (Hill) Lutheran, Berrysburg, Dauphin County, Pennsylvania, USA[227, 228]. Her cause of death was Pilger Fieber u. Kindes Nothen (ie, Pilgrim fever)[228]. She was counted in the census in 1790 in Tulpehocken, Berks County, Pennsylvania, USA (w/father[235]). She was counted in the census in 1800 in Tulpehocken, Berks County, Pennsylvania, USA (w/father[236]). She was counted in the census in 1810 in Upper Paxton, Dauphin County, Pennsylvania, USA (w/father[237]). She was counted in the census in 1820 in Mifflin, Dauphin County, Pennsylvania, USA (w/husband). She was affiliated with the Lutheran religion. She was affiliated with the Reformed religion. She lived in Dauphin County, Pennsylvania, USA between 1816-1824[238].

Susan Gieseman and Adam Frantz had the following children:

    i.   Adam Frantz (son of Adam Frantz and Susan Gieseman) was born in 1811 in Pennsylvania, USA.

    ii.   William Frantz (son of Adam Frantz and Susan Gieseman) was born in 1812 in Pennsylvania, USA. He married Elizabeth ?. She was born in 1812 in Pennsylvania, USA.

    iii.   Jacob Frantz (son of Adam Frantz and Susan Gieseman) was born in 1814 in Pennsylvania, USA.

    iv.   Catherine Frantz (daughter of Adam Frantz and Susan Gieseman) was born about Abt. 1815 in Pennsylvania, USA.

    v.   John Frantz (son of Adam Frantz and Susan Gieseman) was born about Abt. 1815 in Pennsylvania, USA.

    vi.   Christina Frantz (daughter of Adam Frantz and Susan Gieseman) was born in 1818 in Pennsylvania, USA.

15.   vii.   Susan Frantz (daughter of Adam Frantz and Susan Gieseman) was born on March 23, 1819 in Mifflin, Dauphin County, Pennsylvania, USA[62, 123, 125]. She died on October 17, 1861 in Berrysburg, Dauphin County, Pennsylvania, USA[123, 125]. She married Daniel Row (son of John William Rowe and Barbara Rudy) about Abt. 1840 in Dauphin County, Pennsylvania, USA. He was born on July 10, 1813 in Lykens, Dauphin County, Pennsylvania, USA[62, 122, 123, 124]. He died on July 31, 1871 in Berrysburg, Dauphin County, Pennsylvania, USA[123, 124].

    viii.   Sarah Frantz (daughter of Adam Frantz and Susan Gieseman) was born in 1821 in Pennsylvania, USA.

    ix.   Samuel Frantz (son of Adam Frantz and Susan Gieseman) was born in 1824 in Pennsylvania, USA.

Sources

1 Myrtle A. Batdorf birth certificate, January 1918, Department of Vital records, New Castle, PA.

2 Thompson-Batdorf marriage record, Register of Wills, Clerk of Orphans Court, Dauphin Co, PA, 1935.

3 Myrtle Thompson, Obituary, Harrisburg Patriot newspaper, 1983.

4 Myrtle A Thompson death certificate, #3455802, Department of Vital records, New Castle, PA.

5 Samuel Peters, Descendants of John Peters, Evelyn S. Hartman.

6 Harper Bruce Thompson birth record, #344701, #122649-07, September 1907, Schuylkill Co, PA, Department of Vital Records, New Castle, PA.

7 Harper B Thompson death certificate, #2501265, Department of Vital Records, New Castle, PA.

8 Harper B Thompson, Obituary, Harrisburg Patriot Newspaper, July 1981.

9 Myrtle Thompson, Gerald G Thompson.

10 Batdorf household, 1920 United States Census, Dauphin Co, PA, Roll T625 1559, p 3A, ED 148, Image 1081, ancestry.com & Microfilm, PA State Library, Hbg, PA.

11 Batdorf household, 1930 United States Census, Dauphin Co, PA, Roll T626 2027, p 19A, ED 76, Image 0959, ancestry.com & Microfilm, PA State Library, Hbg, PA.

12 Thompson household, US Federal Census 1940, Schuylkill, PA, SD 13, ED 54172, Sh 7A, ancestry.com.

13 Batdorf household, 1930 United States Census, Dauphin Co, PA, Roll T626 2027, p 19A, ED 76, Image 0959, ancestry.com & Microfilm, PA State Library, Hbg, PA.

14 Myrtle A Thompson, Probate files, 1983, File 424-1983, Dauphin County Courthouse, Reg of Wills, Deborah Hershey, Elizabethtown, PA, Mar 2008.

15 Myrtle Thompson, May 1983, PA, Social Security Death Index, www.familysearch.org.

16 Myrtle A Thompson, Obituary, Harrisburg Patriot newspaper, 1983.

17 Thompson household, 1910 United States Census, Schuylkill Co, PA, www.ancestry.com and 1910 United States Census, Schuylkill Co, PA, ED 62, Sheet 32A, PA State Library.

18 Thompson household, 1920 United States Census, Schuylkill Co, PA, Roll T625 1651, ED 84, Image 0280, ancestry.com & Microfilm, PA State Library, Hbg, PA.

19 Thompson household, 1920 United States Census, Schuylkill Co, PA, PA State library, microfilm image.

20 Knittle household, 1930 United States Census, Lehigh Co, PA, ancestry.com & Microfilm, PA State Library, Hbg, PA.

21 Thompson household, 1920 United States Census, Schuylkill Co, PA, Roll T625 1651, ED 84, Image 0280, www.ancestry.com and 1920 United States Census, Schuylkill Co, PA, PA State library, microfilm image.

22 Harper B Thompson, Social Security numident record, application for SS-5, SSA, Nov 2006, Baltimore, MD.

23 Harper Thompson, July 1981, PA, Social Security Death Index, www.familysearch,org.

24 James Edward Batdorf death certificate, #0506183, #66234-39, August 1954, Department of Vital Records, New Castle, PA.

25 James Edward Batdorf, Church record, Rev. O.S. Moyer, Angie Eddy, Maple Grove Cemetery, Eluzabethville, PA, p 29.

26 James Edward Batdorf, United States WW II Draft Reg. Cards, 1942 Record, 2243624, www.ancestry.com.

27 James Edward Batdorf, Social Security numident record, application for SS-5, SSA, Nov 2006, Baltimore, MD.

28 Batdorf-Wert marriage record, Church record, Rev. O.S. Moyer, Angie Eddy, Maple Grove Cemetery, Elizabethville, PA, p 16.

29 Beulah I Batdorf death certificate, #0506188, #057537, June 1983, Department of Vital records, New Castle, PA.

30 Beulah Batdorf, June 1983, PA, Social Security Death Index, www.familysearch.org.

31 Beulah I Batdorf, Obituary, Harrisburg Patriot News, 1983.

32 James Edward Batdorf, Church record, Rev. O.S. Moyer, Angie Eddy, Maple Grove Cemetery, Eluzabethville, PA, p 16.

33 James E Batdorf, Obituary, Harrisburg Patriot news, 1954.

34 Bordorf household, 1900 United States Census, Dauphin Co, PA, T623 1401, p 76, ED 39, sheet 10B, ancestry.com & Microfilm, PA State Library, Hbg, PA.

35 Batdorf household, 1900 United States Census, Dauphin Co, PA, ancestry.com & Microfilm, PA State Library, Hbg, PA.

36 Batdorf household, 1930 United States Census, , PA, Roll T626 2027, p 19A, ED 76, Image 0959, ancestry.com & Microfilm, PA State Library, Hbg, PA.

37 Batdorf household, US Federal Census 1940, Dauphin, PA, SD 19, ED 55-89, Sh 4A, ancestry.com.

38 James Edward Batdorf, World War I Draft Registration Cards, 1917-1918 Record, United States WW II Draft Reg. Cards, 1942 Record, 2243624, www.ancestry.com.

39 James Edward Batdorf, U.S. World War II Draft Registration Cards, 1942, www.ancestry.com.

40 Batdorf household, 1900 United States Census, Dauphin Co, PA, ancestry.com & Microfilm, PA State Library, Hbg, PA.

41 Batdorf household, 1920 United States Census, Dauphin Co, PA, Roll T625 1559, p 3A, ED 148, Image 1081, ancestry.com & Microfilm, PA State Library, Hbg, PA.

42 Batdorf Family information, Mildred Moon, Herndon, PA.

43 James Edward Batdorf, Funeral record copy, John R. Shultz Funeral Home, Lykens, Dauphin Co, PA, 2006, John Shultz, Director.

44 James Edward Batdorf, #0506183, #66234-39, August 1954, Department of Vital Records, New Castle, PA.

45 Wert household, 1900 United States Census, Dauphin Co, PA, www.ancestry.com and 1900 United States Census, Dauphin Co, PA, Pa State Library microfilm image.

46 Beulah I Batdorf, Social Security numident record, application for SS-5, SSA, Nov 2006, Baltimore, MD.

47 John Peters, Peters family information, Evelyn S Hartman, deanh@voicenet.com.

48 Peter Batdorf, Descendants of Peter Batdorf, Evelyn S Hartman, deanh@voicenet.com.

49 Batdorf Family information, Virginia Faust.

50 Thomas Batdorf, #0102590, #81400-17, 1916, Department of Vital records, New Castle, PA.

51 Mary L Batdorf, #0042526, #7?-23, 1924, Department of Vital records, New Castle, PA.

52 Bodorff household, 1860 United States Census, Dauphin Co, PA, ancestry.com & Microfilm, PA State Library, Hbg, PA.

53 Baddorf household, 1870 United States Census, Dauphin Co, PA, ancestry.com & Microfilm, PA State Library, Hbg, PA.

54 Baddorf household, 1880 United States Census, Dauphin Co, PA, FHL 1255124, Film T9-1124, p 246A, www.familysearch.org.

55 Batdorf household, 1910 United States Census, Dauphin Co, PA, ED 120, Sheet 6, ancestry.com & Microfilm, PA State Library, Hbg, PA.

56 Batdorf household, 1910 United States Census, Dauphin Co, PA, ED 120, Sheet 6, ancestry.com & Microfilm, PA State Library, Hbg, PA.

57 Peters household, 1860 United States Census, Dauphin Co, PA, Series M653, Roll 1103, p 568, ancestry.com & Microfilm, PA State Library, Hbg, PA.

58 Batdorf household, 1920 United States Census, Dauphin Co, PA, T625 1557, p 10a, ED 53, Image 0812, ancestry.com & Microfilm, PA State Library, Hbg, PA.

59 Batdorf household, 1920 United States Census, Dauphin Co, PA, T625 1557, p 10a, ED 53, Image 0812, ancestry.com & Microfilm, PA State Library, Hbg, PA.

60 John Wert, #0042527, #95868-1303, 1924, Department of Vital records, New Castle, PA.

61 Adeline Row, St. John Evangelical Lutheran Church, Berrysburg, PA, Sara S. Neagley, Elizabethville, PA.

62 Mrs.. Adeline Wert death certificate, #26162, #3457526, March 1921, Department of Vital Records, New Castle, PA.

63 Descendants of Frederick Adam Faber, Evelyn S Hartman, deanh@voicenet.com.

64 Wert Family, Jonathan Wert.

65 Wert, Sr. household, 1860 United States Census, Northumberland Co, PA, ancestry.com & Microfilm, PA State Library, Hbg, PA.

66 Wert household, 1870 United States Census, Dauphin Co, PA, PA State library microfilm.

67 Wert household, 1880 United States Census, Dauphin Co, PA, FHL 1255124, Film T9-1124, p 251D, www.familysearch.org.

68 Wert household, 1910 United States Census, Dauphin Co, PA, ancestry.com & Microfilm, PA State Library, Hbg, PA.

69 Wert household, 1920 United States Census, Dauphin Co, PA, PA State Library, microfilm image and 1920 United States Census, Dauphin Co, PA, ancestry.com & Microfilm, PA State Library, Hbg, PA.

70 Wert household, 1920 United States Census, Dauphin Co, PA, PA State Library, microfilm image and 1920 United States Census, Dauphin Co, PA, www.ancestry.com.

71 John Henry Wert, Probate files, 1938, #988, Letter of Admin, A 213 21/329, Inv 23 N-512, Dauphin County Courthouse, Reg of Wills, Deborah Hershey, Elizabethtown, PA, Mar 2008.

72 Row household, 1860 United States Census, Dauphin Co, PA, PA State library microfilm.

73 Ely household, 1870 United States Census, Dauphin Co, PA, ancestry.com & Microfilm, PA State Library, Hbg, PA.

74 Michael Goodman, Descendants of Michael Goodman, Evelyn S Hartman, deanh@voicenet.com.

75 Welkers in the USA & Nulls from PA, Greg Welker, gwelker@chesapeake.net, awt.ancestry.com.

76 Baddorf Family, Gratz History, p 193.

77 Peter Batdorf, St. Peters (Hoffmans) Union Church, Burials.

78 Peter Botdorf, St. Peter's (Hoffman's) Union Church, Lykens, Dauphin Co, PA, Gert Mysliwski, gert@foothill.net.

79 Peter Batdorf, Hoffmans Reformed Church, Lykens Valley, Dauphin Co, PA, Historical & Genealogical, pp 227-8.

80 Peter Batdorf, Probate files, 1881, Affidavit Rep #5, Dauphin County Courthouse, Reg of Wills, Deborah Hershey, Elizabethtown, PA, Mar 2008.

81 Elizabeth Batdorf, Hoffmans Reformed Church, Lykens Valley, Dauphin Co, PA, Historical & Genealogical, pp 227-8.

82 Batdorf household, 1820 United States Census, Dauphin Co, PA, ancestry.com & Microfilm, PA State Library, Hbg, PA.

83 Batdorf household, 1830 United States Census, Dauphin Co, PA, ancestry.com & Microfilm, PA State Library, Hbg, PA.

84 Batdorf household, 1840 United States Census, Dauphin Co, PA, ancestry.com & Microfilm, PA State Library, Hbg, PA.

85 Batdorf household, 1840 United States Census, Dauphin Co, PA, PA State library microfilm.

86 Bottorff household, 1850 United States Census, Dauphin Co, PA, Roll M432-775, [age 399, Image 363, ancestry.com & Microfilm, PA State Library, Hbg, PA.

87 Baddorf household, 1870 United States Census, Dauphin Co, PA, PA State library microfilm.

88 Batdorf household, 1880 United States Census, Dauphin Co, PA, Roll T9-1124, p 57A, ED 106, Image 0924, ancestry.com & Microfilm, PA State Library, Hbg, PA.

89 Welker household, 1820 United States Census, Dauphin Co, PA, ancestry.com & Microfilm, PA State Library, Hbg, PA.

90 Welker household, 1830 United States Census, Dauphin Co, PA, ancestry.com & Microfilm, PA State Library, Hbg, PA.

91 John Welker, Welker family, Gratz History, p 450-455.

92 Mary Peters death certificate, bk C, #945, 1897, Dauphin County Register of Wills, Harrisburg, PA.

93 Mary Peters death certificate, Dauphin County Register of Wills, bk C, #945, 1897, Harrisburg, PA. Source 140, bk C, #945, 1897, Perry County Historians.

94 Mary Peters death certificate, Dauphin County Register of Wills, bk C, #945, 1897, Harrisburg, PA.

95 Peters household, 1830 United States Census, Union Co, PA, ancestry.com & Microfilm, PA State Library, Hbg, PA.

96 John Peters, Year: 1840; Census Place: Buffalo, Union, Pennsylvania; Roll: 496; Page: 310; Image: 640; Family History Library Film: 0020558.

97 Peters household, 1850 United States Census, Dauphin Co, PA, Pam Patton, poohie@penn.com.

98 Peters household, 1850 United States Census, Dauphin Co, PA, FTM CD305, Disk 10, film 831.

99 Mary Peters death certificate, Mary Peters death record, bk C, #945, 1897, Dauphin County Register of Wills, Harrisburg, PA.

100 John Swartz, 1820 U S Census; Census Place: Juniata, Perry, Pennsylvania; Page: 353; NARA Roll: M33_104; Image: 347.

101 Swartz household, 1830 United States Census, Perry Co, PA, ancestry.com & Microfilm, PA State Library, Hbg, PA.

102 John Swartz, Year: 1830; Census Place: Juniata, Perry, Pennsylvania; Series: M19; Roll: 156; Page: 284; Family History Library Film: 0020630.

103 Swartz household, 1840 United States Census, Perry Co, PA, ancestry.com & Microfilm, PA State Library, Hbg, PA.

104 Peters household, 1870 United States Census, Dauphin Co, PA, Series M593, Roll 1335 p 538, ancestry.com & Microfilm, PA State Library, Hbg, PA.

105 Row household, 1880 United States Census, Dauphin Co, PA, FHLF 1255124, NA film T9-1124, p 245c, ancestry.com & Microfilm, PA State Library, Hbg, PA.

106 David Wert death certificate, Dauphin County Register of Wills, bk E, #852, December 20, 1900, , Harrisburg, PA.

107 Shoop family information, Are you my cousin, Howard Ward, haroldw1@juno.com, awt.ancestry.com.

108 Monn & Related Families, Danni Monn Hopkins, clueless@clnk.com, awt.ancestry.com.

109 David Wert (West) death record, Extract from County Death records, 1893-1906.

110 Wertz family information, Bob Messerschmidt, Laurel, MD, SusanM4383@aol.com.

111 Wertz family information, Cindi Grimm, Grimm@ruralife.net.

112 Shoop family information, Are you my cousin, Harold Ward, haroldw1@juno.com, awt.ancestry.com.

113 David Wert, Wiconisco Calvary Cemetery.

114 David Wert, Dauphin County Register of Wills, bk E, #852, December 20, 1900, , Harrisburg, PA.

115 Wert household, 1830 United States Census, Dauphin Co, PA, ancestry.com & Microfilm, PA State Library, Hbg, PA.

116 Wert household, 1840 United States Census, Dauphin Co, PA, ancestry.com & Microfilm, PA State Library, Hbg, PA.

117 Wert household, 1850 United States Census, Dauphin Co, PA, PA State library microfilm.

118 Schamper?/Buffington household, 1850 United States Census, Dauphin Co, PA, PA State library microfilm.

119 Shoop household, 1840 United States Census, Northumberland Co, PA, ancestry.com & Microfilm, PA State Library, Hbg, PA.

120 Shoop household, 1850 United States Census, Northumberland Co, PA, ancestry.com & Microfilm, PA State Library, Hbg, PA.

121 Catherine Wert, Probate files, 1880, A-3, Dauphin County Courthouse, Reg of Wills, Deborah Hershey, Elizabethtown, PA, Mar 2008.

122 Daniel Row, Baptismal record, St. John Evangelical Lutheran Church, Dauphin Co, PA, p 64.

123 Rowe family information, Howard E Row, Dover, DE.

124 Daniel Rowe, St. John Evangelical Lutheran Church, Berrysburg, PA, Sara S. Neagley, Elizabethville, PA, 424 6M 24D.

125 Susanna Rowe, St. John Evangelical Lutheran Church, Berrysburg, PA, Sara S. Neagley, Elizabethville, PA.

126 Row household, 1820 United States Census, Dauphin Co, PA, ancestry.com & Microfilm, PA State Library, Hbg, PA.

127 Row household, 1830 United States Census, Dauphin Co, PA, ancestry.com & Microfilm, PA State Library, Hbg, PA.

128 Rowe household, 1840 United States Census, Dauphin Co, PA, ancestry.com & Microfilm, PA State Library, Hbg, PA.

129 Rowe household, 1840 United States Census, Dauphin Co, PA, PA State library microfilm.

130 Row household, 1850 United States Census, Dauphin Co, PA, PA State library microfilm.

131 Row household, 1860 United States Census, Dauphin Co, PA, ancestry.com & Microfilm, PA State Library, Hbg, PA.

132 Zerber household, 1870 United States Census, Dauphin Co, PA, PA State library microfilm.

133 Daniel Row, Probate files, 1871, Letter of Admin, Dauphin County Courthouse, Reg of Wills, Deborah Hershey, Elizabethtown, PA, Mar 2008.

134 Susanna Rowe, St. John Evangelical Lutheran Church, Berrysburg, PA, Sara S. Neagley, Elizabethville, PA, 424 6M 24D.

135 Frantz household, 1820 United States Census, Dauphin Co, PA, ancestry.com & Microfilm, PA State Library, Hbg, PA.

136 Peter Batdorf, Descendants of Peter Batdorf, Evelyn S. Hartman.

137 Pottorff household, 1800 United States Federal Census, Dauphin Co, PA, ancestry.com & Microfilm, PA State Library, Hbg, PA.

138 Badorf Jr household, 1820 United States Census, Dauphin Co, PA, ancestry.com & Microfilm, PA State Library, Hbg, PA.

139 Badorf Jr household, 1820 United States Census, Dauphin Co, PA, PA State Library microfilm.

140 Peter Batdorf, Probate files, 1829, Letter of Admin, P248 A, Dauphin County Courthouse, Reg of Wills, Deborah Hershey, Elizabethtown, PA, Mar 2008.

141 Dauphin County Names, Data p, www://genealogy.lv/howard/.

142 Baddorf household, 1830 United States Census, Dauphin Co, PA, PA State library microfilm.

143 Baddorf household, 1830 United States Census, Dauphin Co, PA, ancestry.com & Microfilm, PA State Library, Hbg, PA.

144 Batrdorf household, 1830 United States Census, Dauphin Co, PA, ancestry.com & Microfilm, PA State Library, Hbg, PA.

145 Valentine Welker, Direct Descendants of Valentine (Welcher) Welker, Evelyn S. Hartman.

146 Dauphin County Names, Data p, Robert M Howard, www://genealogy.lv/howard/.

147 Welker family information, Roger Cramer, rogercubs@aol.com.

148 John Welker, U.S., Find A Grave Index, 1600s-Current, Ancestry.com. U.S., Find A Grave Index, 1600s-Current [database on-line]. Provo, UT, USA: Ancestry.com Operations, Inc., 012. Original data: Find A Grave. Find A Grave. http://www.findagrave.com/cgi-bin/fg.cgi.

149 Welker Family, Gratz History, p 450-455.

150 Pats Family, Pat Scott, pat.scott@comcast.net, awt.ancestry.com.

151 Elizabeth Messerschmidt, Pennsylvania Church Records - Adams, Berks, and Lancaster Counties, 1729-1881 about Elizabeth Messerschmidt.

152 John Welker, Barbara Brady O'Keefe, 2120 SW 127 Avenue, Miami, FL & Cindy Maloney, cynwelker8@rurelated.com.

153 Welker household, 1790 United States Census, Dauphin Co, PA, ancestry.com & Microfilm, PA State Library, Hbg, PA.

154 Welker household, 1800 United States Census, Dauphin Co, PA, ancestry.com & Microfilm, PA State Library, Hbg, PA.

155 Welker household, 1821 United States Census, Dauphin Co, PA, Roll M252 54m p 538, Image 123, ancestry.com & Microfilm, PA State Library, Hbg, PA.

156 Welker household, 1820 United States Census, Dauphin Co, PA, PA State library microfilm.

157 Welker household, 1830 United States Census, Dauphin Co, PA, PA State library microfilm.

158 Welker household, 1840 United States Census, Dauphin Co, PA, ancestry.com & Microfilm, PA State Library, Hbg, PA.

159 Welker household, 1840 United States Census, Dauphin Co, PA, PA State library microfilm.

160 Welker household, 1850 United States Census, Dauphin Co, PA, ancestry.com & Microfilm, PA State Library, Hbg, PA.

161 John Welker, Probate files, 1854, F-413-4, Dauphin County Courthouse, Reg of Wills, Deborah Hershey, Elizabethtown, PA, Mar 2008.

162 Messerschmidt household, 1800 United States Census, Dauphin Co, PA, ancestry.com & Microfilm, PA State Library, Hbg, PA.

163 Peters Research, Michael McCormick, Enduring Legacy, Gardners, PA, Feb 2009.

164 Peters household, 1850 United States Federal Census, Union, PA, 288, ancestry.com & Microfilm, PA State Library, Hbg, PA.

165 Maria Peters, Death notice, Lewisburg Chronicle, Oct. 1852 c/o Union County Historical Society, Maggie Miller, hstorici@ptd.net.

166 John Peters, Year: 1800; Census Place: East Buffalo, Northumberland, Pennsylvania; Series: M32; Roll: 37; Page: 724; Image: 141; Family History Library Film: 363340.

167 Peters household, 1810 United States Census, Northumberland Co, PA, ancestry.com & Microfilm, PA State Library, Hbg, PA.

168 Peters household, 1820 United States Census, Union Co, PA, ancestry.com & Microfilm, PA State Library, Hbg, PA.

169 John Peters Jr, Year: 1830; Census Place: Buffalo, Union, Pennsylvania; Series: M19; Roll: 149; Page: 346; Family History Library Film: 0020623.

170 Maria Peters, Death notice, Lewisburg Chronicle, octo. 1852 c/o Union County Historical Society, Maggie Miller, hstorici@ptd.net.

171 Swartz household, 1820 US Federal Census, Juniata, Perry Co, PA, www.ancestry.com.

172 John Smarty [John Swartz], Year: 1840; Census Place: Juniata, Perry, Pennsylvania; Roll: 480; Page: 340; Image: 687; Family History Library Film: 0020553.

173 Jacob Wert, Wert family, Onetree, ancestry.com.

174 Elizabeth Wert death record, Extract from County Death records, 1893-1906.

175 Jacob Wert, HSMUP, Mbg, PA 17061, via mail, not dated or cited.

176 Wert household, 1810 United States Census, Dauphin Co, PA, ancestry.com & Microfilm, PA State Library, Hbg, PA.

177 Wert household, 1820 United States Census, Dauphin Co, PA, ancestry.com & Microfilm, PA State Library, Hbg, PA.

178 Wert household, 1830 United States Census, Dauphin Co, PA ancestry.com & Microfilm, PA State Library, Hbg, PA.

179 Wert household, 1830 United States Census, Dauphin Co, PA, PA State library microfilm.

180 Jacob West, Year: 1840; Census Place: Jackson, Dauphin, Pennsylvania; Roll: 456; Page: 329; Image: 678; Family History Library Film: 0020543.

181 Wirt household, 1860 United States Census, Dauphin Co, PA, PA State library microfilm.

182 Wert household, 1870 United States Census, Lehigh Co, PA, ancestry.com.

183 Wert household, 1870 United States Census, Lehigh Co, PA, ancestry.com.

184 Wert Family.

185 Sarah Elizabeth Faber Wert, HSMUP, Mbg, PA 17061, via mail, not dated or cited.

186 Faber household, 1810 United States Census, Dauphin Co, PA, ancestry.com & Microfilm, PA State Library, Hbg, PA.

187 Faber household, 1820 United States Census, Dauphin Co, PA, ancestry.com & Microfilm, PA State Library, Hbg, PA.

188 Wert, Sr. household, 1870 United States Census, Roll M593 1335, p 649, Image 420, ancestry.com & Microfilm, PA State Library, Hbg, PA.

189 Harman household, 1870 United States Census, Roll M593 1335, p 649, Image 420, ancestry.com & Microfilm, PA State Library, Hbg, PA.

190 Shoop family information, Northumberland Co County, PA 1777-1865, Stone Valley Lutheran, www.ancestry.com.

191 Johannes Schup, Stone Valley Cemetery, Robert Straub, Dalmatia, PA, Section A, Row 16, Grave 30.

192 Wert Family, Jonathan Wert, www.mdi-wert.com.

193 Sarah Wertz, David C Paul, Owner: dcpnascar7781, ancestry.com.

194 Shoop household, 1810 United States Census, Dauphin Co, PA, ancestry.com & Microfilm, PA State Library, Hbg, PA.

195 Shoop household, 1820 United States Census, Dauphin Co, PA, ancestry.com & Microfilm, PA State Library, Hbg, PA.

196 Shoop household, 1830 United States Census, Northumberland Co, PA, ancestry.com & Microfilm, PA State Library, Hbg, PA.

197 Shoop household, 1850 United States Census, Dauphin Co, PA, ancestry.com & Microfilm, PA State Library, Hbg, PA.

198 John Shoop, Probate files, 1862, Northumberland County Courthouse, Reg of Wills, Sunbury, Bk B, p629, PA, Robyn Jackson, genealogylover@msn.com, 2008.

199 Wertz household, 1820 United States Census, Northumberland Co, PA, ancestry.com & Microfilm, PA State Library, Hbg, PA.

200 The Lunnys, William Lunny, rlunny@msn.com, awt.ancestry.com.

201 Frank Rowe, FHL, Pedigree chart, www.familysearch.org.

202 William Rowe, Family Data Collection, Individual Records, www.ancestry.com, Edmund West, comp.

203 William Rowe, Rowe family, Onetree, ancestry.com.

204 William Rowe, Descendants of Frank (Rau) Rowe, Evelyn S. Hartman.

205 William Rowe, St. John Evangelical Lutheran Church, Berrysburg, PA, Sara S. Neagley, Elizabethville, PA, 424 6M 24D.

206 Rowe household, 1790 United States Census, Lancaster Co, PA, ancestry.com & Microfilm, PA State Library, Hbg, PA.

207 Rowe household, 1800 United States Census, Lancaster Co, PA, ancestry.com & Microfilm, PA State Library, Hbg, PA.

208 Rowe household, 1820 United States Census, Dauphin Co, PA, ancestry.com & Microfilm, PA State Library, Hbg, PA.

209 Rowe household, 1820 United States Census, Dauphin Co, PA, PA State library microfilm.

210 Rowe household, 1830 United States Census, Dauphin Co, PA, ancestry.com & Microfilm, PA State Library, Hbg, PA.

211 Rowe household, 1830 United States Census, Dauphin Co, PA, PA State library microfilm.

212 Row household, 1840 United States Census, Dauphin Co, PA, ancestry.com & Microfilm, PA State Library, Hbg, PA.

213 Row household, 1850 United States Census, Dauphin Co, PA, ancestry.com & Microfilm, PA State Library, Hbg, PA.

214 Row household, 1870 United States Census, Dauphin Co, PA, Roll M593-1335, p 710, Image 542, ancestry.com & Microfilm, PA State Library, Hbg, PA.

215 Rosie household, 1820 United States Census, Dauphin Co, PA, ancestry.com & Microfilm, PA State Library, Hbg, PA.

216 Row household, 1850 United States Census, Dauphin Co, PA, ancestry.com & Microfilm, PA State Library, Hbg, PA.

217 Rau/Row, PA Births, Dauphin County, J. Humphrey.

218 William Row, Probate files, 1873, Letter of Admin, Dauphin County Courthouse, Reg of Wills, Deborah Hershey, Elizabethtown, PA, Mar 2008.

219 Barbara Rowe, St. John Evangelical Lutheran Church, Berrysburg, PA, Sara S. Neagley, Elizabethville, PA, 424 6M 24D.

220 Rudy household, 1800 United States Census, Lancaster Co, PA, ancestry.com & Microfilm, PA State Library, Hbg, PA.

221 Row household, 1880 United States Census, Dauphin Co, PA, FHL 1255124, Film T9-1124, p 244A, www.familysearch.org.

222 Johann Wilhelm Frantz, Descendants of Johann Wilhelm Frantz, Evelyn S. Hartman.

223 Adam Frantz, Frantz family, Onetree, ancestry.com.

224 Gieseman family information, Mary Smith.

225 Franz-Gieseman marriage record, October 1811, source unknown.

226 Susanna Franz, St. John's Congr., 17 feb 1826, Mifflin, Dauphin Co, PA, Gert, gert@foothill.net.

227 Franz-Gieseman marriage record, October 1811, Lykens Valley lower church (David's Reformed) Millersburg, Upper Paxton, Dauphin Co, 1774-1844.

228 Susanna Franz, St. John's Congr., 17 feb 1826, Mifflin, Dauphin Co, PA, Gert Mysliwski, gert@foothill.net.

229 Frantz household, 1790 United States Census, Lancaster Co, PA, ancestry.com & Microfilm, PA State Library, Hbg, PA.

230 Frantz household, 1800 United States Census, Dauphin Co, PA, ancestry.com & Microfilm, PA State Library, Hbg, PA.

231 Frontz household, 1820 United States Census, Dauphin Co, PA, ancestry.com & Microfilm, PA State Library, Hbg, PA.

232 Adam Frantz, Dauphin County, Pennnsylavnia, 1800-55, St. Peters (Hoffmans) Church, Lykens, Dauphin Co, PA, www.ancestry.com.

233 Adam Frantz, War of 1812 Records, DDC, 1999-, www.ancestry.com.

234 Frontz household, 1820 United States Census, Dauphin Co, PA, ancestry.com & Microfilm, PA State Library, Hbg, PA.

235 Gieseman household, 1790 United States Census, Berks Co, PA, ancestry.com & Microfilm, PA State Library, Hbg, PA.

236 Gieseman household, 1800 United States Census, Berks Co, PA, ancestry.com & Microfilm, PA State Library, Hbg, PA.

237 Geseman household, 1810 United States Census, Dauphin Co, PA, ancestry.com & Microfilm, PA State Library, Hbg, PA.

238 Susanna Frantz, Dauphin County, Pennnsylavnia, 1800-55, St. Peters (Hoffmans) Church, Lykens, Dauphin Co, PA, www.ancestry.com.

NARRATIVE SOURCES

www.pbs.org/wned/war-of-1812/timeline/

Lykens-Williams Valley history - directory and pictorial review.

Estimated from information found at http://www.carnegielibrary.org/research/

Lykens-Williams Valley history - directory and pictorial review

http://www.wtwp.org/

Harrisburg Patriot, January 18, 1906

Harrisburg Patriot, August 24, 1906

http://www.familysearch.org

Harrisburg Patriot, August 23, 1917

Lykens - Williams Valley History Directory J. Allen Barrett

ancestry.com

http://archive.org/stream/lykenswilliamsva00barr/lykenswilliamsva00barr_djvu.txt

http://www.dol.gov/dol/aboutdol/history/coalstrike.htm

http://www.portal.state.pa.us/portal/server.pt/community/events/4279/

http://www.msha.gov/District/Dist_01/History/history.htm

http://archive.org/stream/lykenswilliamsva00barr/lykenswilliamsva00barr_djvu.txt

Harrisburg Patriot Sept. 7, 1891

http://archive.org/stream/lykenswilliamsva00barr/lykenswilliamsva00barr_djvu.txt

http://archive.org/stream/lykenswilliamsva00barr/lykenswilliamsva00barr_djvu.txt

http://archive.org/stream/lykenswilliamsva00barr/lykenswilliamsva00barr_djvu.txt

http://www.dol.gov/dol/aboutdol/history/coalstrike.htm

http://www.portal.state.pa.us/portal/server.pt/community/events/4279/

http://www.msha.gov/District/Dist_01/History/history.htm

http://archive.org/stream/lykenswilliamsva00barr/lykenswilliamsva00barr_djvu.txt

Harrisburg Patriot Sept. 7, 1891

http://archive.org/stream/lykenswilliamsva00barr/lykenswilliamsva00barr_djvu.txt

http://archive.org/stream/lykenswilliamsva00barr/lykenswilliamsva00barr_djvu.txt

Lykens-Williams Valley directory and pictorial review

Map population density of the United States from the 1810 census

www.wfu.edu

Lykens-Williams Valley directory and pictorial review

Annals of Buffalo Valley, Pennsylvania, 1755-1855, Linn, John Blair

www.unioncountyhistoricalsociety.orgAnnals of Buffalo Valley, Pennsylvania, 1755-1855 Linn, John Blair

1850 United States Census

Annals of Buffalo Valley, Pennsylvania, 1755-1855 Linn, John Blair

Lykens-Williams Valley history - directory and pictorial review.

http://archive.org/stream/lykenswilliamsva00barr/lykenswilliamsva00barr_djvu.txt

http://www.dcnr.state.pa.us/cs/groups/public/documents/document/dcnr_009325.pdf

http://explorepahistory.com/story.php?storyId=1-9-E&chapter=1 (Dauphinfrom state data)

http://www.dcnr.state.pa.us/cs/groups/public/documents/document/dcnr_009325.pdf

ABOUT THE AUTHORS

Marc D. Thompson delved into writing and genealogy at a very early age. He wrote stories, poems, lyrics and family history books. Marc went on to write and research in high school and college, earning a BS degree from Moravian College. He has presented genealogical lectures and authored over ten family history volumes. Marc's other published works include The Fitness Book of Lists, Virtual Personal Training Manual, Fitness Quotes of Humorous Inspiration and a poetry compilation, He currently pens a genealogy blog at google blogger and wrote a monthly genealogy column for Atlantic Avenue Magazine. He is a member of the Association of Professional Genealogists, founded a PA Genealogy Society and was the County Coordinator of the Chatham Co, GA USGenweb site. Marc believes in what he calls Creatalytical Thinking: The fusion of creativity and analysis to view life more fully and fulfill his place in this world. Writing now for over four decades, Marc has been influenced by science, art and his relationships, and yet marvels at the cosmically-driven direction he receives from energy around him.

Jack Smiles is retired community newspaper writer and editor in Pennsylvania. He has sold articles to Pennsylvania Magazine, Antique Week, Sports Collector's Digest, Ambassador Magazine and several newspapers. He has had baseball-themed fiction published in Spitball Magazine and Minor Trips. He is the author of three biographies of Pennsylvania coal miners turned Hall of Fame baseball players: EE-Yah, the Life and Times of Hughie Jennings; Big Ed Walsh: the Life and Times of a Spitballing Hall of Famer and Bucky Harris: a Biography of Baseball's Boy Wonder, all published by McFarland. Mr. Smiles, 60, resides in Wyoming, Pennsylvania, and can be reached at jsmiles9@gmail.com.

INDEX OF INDIVIDUALS

INDEX OF INDIVIDUALS

INDEX OF INDIVIDUALS